BECOME A RICHER YOU:

ONE BOOK, ONE SYSTEM, ONE HABIT

LIFESUCCESS PUBLISHING, LLC
8900 E Pinnacle Peak Road, Suite D240
Scottsdale, AZ 85255

Telephone:	800.473.7134
Fax:	480.661.1014
E-mail:	admin@lifesuccesspublishing.com
ISBN:	978-1-59930-165-5
Cover :	Daniela A. Savone, LifeSuccess Publishing, LLC
Text:	Daniela A. Savone, LifeSuccess Publishing, LLC

COMPANIES, ORGANIZATIONS, INSTITUTIONS, AND INDUSTRY PUBLICATIONS: Quantity discounts are available on bulk purchases of this book for reselling, educational purposes, subscription incentives, gifts, sponsorship, or fundraising. Special books or book excerpts can also be created to fit specific needs such as private labeling with your logo on the cover and a message from a VIP printed inside. For more information, please contact our Special Sales Department at LifeSuccess Publishing, LLC.

Printed in Canada.

BECOME A RICHER YOU:

ONE BOOK, ONE SYSTEM, ONE HABIT

DOUG MEHARG

CONTENTS

ACKNOWLEDGMENTS

I committed to writing a book years ago. I even paid for it years ago. I never quite got around to it though. All that changed when I realized that kids need to understand better money management to live and thrive in the new global economy. An idea was hatched, and I put pen to paper.

For those of you who know me, you also know that writing does not come easily to me. Fortunately, I was able to gather a great team together and build this manuscript from my thoughts, ideas, and, mainly, from the mission of my new company, Kids Ride to Riches.

My team was graced by my family, especially my two daughters. Thanks to Angela for transcribing my handwritten chapters and emailing them to my writer, Dianne Sagan. My gratitude also goes to Sarah for her support and encouragement to get this manuscript ready. Sarah picked my brain, adjusted the details in the stories (some of which were seventy years old!), and made sure the story I tell in these pages is my own. She was a great support to me during the project.

My heartfelt thanks also go to my wife, Johanna, for supporting me throughout this project.

It has been a pleasure corresponding with Dianne Sagan for the duration of the first draft of this book. She did a great job putting everything in order to make this an interesting book for parents and kids.

I give deep thanks to my mother who showed me that when I put my mind to something, I could get it done.

I am grateful for all the people throughout my life who have challenged me and motivated me to learn. Thank you, Bob Proctor, for the lessons of a lifetime.

I also want to thank Harry James, who collaborated with me on this book, and his staff, in particular Sian and Elizabeth, who typed from my handwritten notes.

FOREWORD

It's always refreshing when you can confirm consistency between what someone says and how he lives his life. There is no shortage of people who have preached one thing, yet lived another—from the divorced psychologist promoting his book on how to create a successful marriage, to the fitness guru who smokes behind the shed! Not Doug Meharg, though.

At age seventy-seven, Doug has a solid track record of practicing what he preaches when it comes to money and true financial freedom.

What is most refreshing is how Doug has channeled his entrepreneurial spirit into a vision of raising a generation of kids who are truly financially liberated. Doug has observed, like many of us, that the educational system—from grade one to college—does a lousy job preparing our kids for the financial world in which they live. Unfortunately, most of the time our kids are competing against multinational companies that are very good at putting them on financial treadmills made of plastic cards and deferred payment schemes.

The institutions know that a person's greatest financial asset is his ability to earn an income. Their goal, of course, is to have as much of that income as possible diverted to them for mortgage payments, credit card payments, and loans for that expensive new car. The companies' shareholders flourish at our kids' expense. The sad truth is that our children are mortgaging their future to live their material dreams today; the irony is, however, that by buying into this form of financial slavery, they are actually giving away their future. Our kids have to differentiate wants from needs and take ownership of their own financial destinies. In other words, our kids have to become equipped to make good decisions and understand the concept that their *income* should dictate their *lifestyle*, not the other way around!

They need to be liberated by the fact that if they buy into some very basic—but true—financial laws, the sky can be the limit, no matter what they do for a living. They can pursue their passion *and* become financially independent. The widely accepted financial malady of having lifestyle dictate income is suppressing our kids and stealing their dreams. More important, the stress is affecting their health, and as many statistics confirm, that same stress is ruining their marriages and futures.

Why? How did we get here? Why isn't somebody doing something about it? This mind-set is so prevalent and so accepted that most people have learned to live with this financial stress instead of doing something about it.

Generations of parents have passed down some poor financial management skills, and their children have picked up some bad habits by observing their parents. I'm not suggesting that it's the parents' fault; they did the best they could based on what they were taught.

For most of us, managing money was trial and error: work hard at school, get a job, and then walk into the local bank with absolutely no financial skills whatsoever and buy a $300,000 house. The bank doesn't ask if you like skydiving or how often you like to go out for dinner. Oh no, the bank has debt-servicing ratios that assume your favorite meal consists of six almonds and a glass of water. Of course, you discovered this when you were trying to figure out how to make your second mortgage payment.

Your neighbour could see your stress right through your front window because you couldn't afford window coverings! "No problem," you thought to yourself. "I'll make up the shortfall with a credit card cash advance, and somehow I'll balance it next month." The problem was that your wife wasn't happy with the Canadian flag hanging in the front window, so she put some very nice curtains on the credit card. Before you knew it, you were under such a mountain of debt that your goal became survival, let alone becoming financially secure.

I'm shocked that one of the main goals I hear from many people is, "I just want to get out of debt." It's interesting that they don't say, "I'd like to be a millionaire" or "I'd like to buy an investment property in Europe" or "I'd like to start my own business."

No, our personal financial mismanagement in this country has become such a mess that the key to life is to get out of debt. Part of this book emphasizes the natural law that whatever we focus on increases. So if we are focused on being debt free—guess what? We may just get more of the same. *Debt.*

Doug Meharg, the author of *Become a Richer You*, and I have spent many hours debating these points, and I have also had the privilege of working with him on one of his Kids Ride to Riches seminars. Doug is not naïve enough to think he can teach families good money management skills overnight, nor does he believe he has all the answers. However, like anyone who has accomplished anything worthwhile, Doug's passion is contagious.

At a Kids Ride to Riches seminar, I saw the kids become spellbound as Doug gave them real-life examples of money management and becoming a millionaire based on his experiences. The most common comment from all of the kids after the seminars is that they thought it was going to be boring because we were talking about money. However, they said the seminar left them empowered with some basic financial tools and they felt ready to take on Donald Trump!

For me, the most potent aspect of Doug's message was illuminated when a young lad asked if he could still be financially successful if he pursued his dream of becoming a carpenter. As Doug explained to the boy that he could accomplish both goals, I watched as the boy sat up and straightened his shoulders. It so happened that these young carpenter's ambitions were Doug's own humble beginnings.

Our kids have been sold a bill of goods and filled with preconceived notions that are just plain false. You don't have to be a doctor, lawyer, or dentist to be financially successful in life. As a matter of fact, in more than twenty years of financial practice in this country, I have never observed any direct correlation between occupation and financial success. I have, however, seen many people from many different walks of life benefit from the basic financial laws that anyone can embrace. These laws are outlined in this book.

I mentioned that many people have observed the poor financial education our children receive. As a parent of four children, I want to express my sincere gratitude to Doug for taking action. Doug's talent, track record, and skill set could be used a thousand different ways, but he has chosen to lay a path for a brighter, more liberated financial future for our kids by writing this book.

Become a Richer You: A Family's Guide to Success plants the seeds. After reading this book and practicing the Kids Ride to Riches skills, our kids may begin giving some sage financial advice to their parents!

Harry James is an entrepreneur with business interests in everything from real estate to aggregates. As one of Canada's top financial advisors, he is a sought-after speaker.

INTRODUCTION

This book, *Become a Richer You: A Family's Guide to Success*, is a guide for families that, if followed, will change your children's futures—for the better. And isn't this what we truly want for our children? For our collective futures?

I have written this book with our children's futures in mind. I'm an experienced entrepreneur, businessman, author, and speaker. I founded Kids Ride to Riches (www.kidsridetoriches.com), a program that enables families to learn together and young people to learn the secrets of the wealthy. My company teaches that wealth and riches are not just about money, but that money is a part of living rich in all aspects of being.

I know that money is one of the last taboo subjects. Most people don't have the capacity or belief system to properly convey good money management skills to their children. Most people have the best of intentions, but their religious beliefs and social conditioning often make *money* the subject of hushed and private conversations—never to be shared with children. Even I fell into this trap when I was a young parent. I didn't understand how to convey my knowledge to my children, and because I had been trained to conduct financial transactions privately, my children never learned by example how I became a millionaire.

Well, those days are long gone. I made a commitment to teach the next generation about riches and how to have them. This book is an outcome of my commitment.

What if there were a way to have good conversations about money with your kids? There is a way, and I have written this book as a helpful guide for you to follow.

To begin, I firmly believe that you are reading this book for a reason. To better understand your own reasons, I have created a series of introspective questions that you can ask yourself in approximately five minutes. These questions are meant to get you thinking about what you are *currently* doing and what you *need* to do for you and your family to learn money management skills and how to be become a richer you. These questions are meant to help you form a checklist of those things you'll need to pay particular attention to in this book. The checklist will help you see how you are doing and how you can improve. It doesn't matter where you start. It only matters where you go from here.

1. Would you like to get out of debt and be able to pay all of your bills?

2. Do you have a savings account? How often do you put money in savings?

3. Do you currently have any investments? What are they?

4. How much do you make from your investments monthly?

5. On a scale of 1–10 (10 representing extreme, debilitating stress), what level of stress regarding money and finances do you consistently experience?

6. On a scale of 1–10 (10 representing extreme, debilitating stress), what level of stress regarding money and finances do you think your children consistently experience?

7. On a scale of 1–10 (10 representing extreme, debilitating stress), what level of stress regarding money and finances do you think your spouse/partner consistently experiences?

8. Do you currently live primarily paycheck to paycheck?

9. When you think or talk about money, do you have a positive or a negative attitude?

10. If you were provided with a fun, interactive series of activities related to money, finances, attitude, and goal setting, what is the likelihood that you would complete the activities with your family?

11. Do you work for someone?

12. Do you have your own business?

13. Write down three goals that you have regarding money and finances.

14. How did your parents educate you about money and finances? How about your grandparents?

15. If you have children, what have you taught them about money and finances that was different from your own training in this area? How has your family been progressing in this area?

16. Would you like your children to learn money management skills that will make them successful and wealthy?

17. What is in your library regarding money, finances, and other topics related to becoming a richer you?

Thank you for taking the time to answer these questions. You now have your starting point and a snapshot of where you are regarding money and finances.

This book begins with principles. Have you ever asked yourself why some people are wealthy and can do anything they want, while others seem to struggle from paycheck to paycheck? The answers are in the following pages and are a great first step to giving your children the ability to *be, do, and have* anything they want in life. And you can, too.

You will learn the basic money management lessons that have been taught to the wealthiest people in the world—handed down from parent to child. Now is your opportunity to give your children the gift of riches. Learn, as a family, how to manage money and create riches together.

Become a part of the learning process. Find the richest you, and gift your children with a legacy of riches. This guide is easy to read, so you'll put these lessons to work and help your children discover that everyone is born rich!

HOW TO READ THIS BOOK

"Part I: How to Become a Richer You" covers the knowledge and skills necessary to become rich. At the end of each chapter, you'll see a summary of the main points discussed in that chapter. These summaries are called "Family Success Checklists." If you're like my own grown kids, they don't have a lot of time to read, so these summaries may be of great importance to you.

"Part II: Let's Do ... Become a Richer You" includes the activities that you need to complete in order to practice the knowledge and skills to become rich. These chapters and activities are directly related to the knowledge and skills covered in Part I. You can refer back and forth between the two parts.

If you are a parent and are involving your family in the discussion of money and finances (congratulations, by the way!), you can read the Part I chapters alone and then lead your family in some of the activities and discussions in Part II. This way you'll know a little bit more about some of the topics and can facilitate the discussion.

If you're not a parent, just read the whole book and do the activities!

Remember that doing the activities is the part that most people skip. Only 2 percent of people will take the advice in this book, do the activities, and implement the knowledge and skills in their own lives. These are the people who often become financially free. These are the lifelong learners of our society. Why is it that when people recommend a book, a course, or other life-improving opportunity, most of us turn it down? We tell ourselves we'll get to it later.

Guess what? You won't get to it later.

Do the activities now. Together.

Enjoy this book and let me know what you think: doug@kidsridetoriches.com.

ACTIVITY: MY FAMILY'S FINANCIAL AWARENESS

Understanding your own level of financial awareness is the key to identifying what else you need to know to achieve your financial goals. This activity will help you focus your attention on gaining the skills available to you in this book. Being aware is a big part of financial smarts.

The answer key is found in Appendix B. Make this activity fun! You can do this activity alone; however, I suggest that you do it as a family activity because then you will assess your knowledge together.

INSTRUCTIONS:

1. Gather your family together; ask them if they would like to participate in this financial awareness activity.

2. Get their agreement to participate.

3. Read the first question out loud.

4. Give each person a chance to answer.

5. At the end of the activity, discuss some of the differences and similarities that came up in your answers.

MULTIPLE CHOICE: PICK THE BEST ANSWER.

1. What percent of people worry about money every day?

   a. 90 percent

   √ b. 70 percent √

   c. 50 percent

2. What percent of people live paycheck to paycheck?

   a. 85 percent

   b. 79 percent

   c. 66 percent √

3. Do people save more or less money now than they did ten years ago?

   √ a. Less √

   b. More

   c. About the same

4. The use of savings accounts is more prevalent in
    _____ c _____ than _____ d _____.

    a. the UK; Canada

    b. Canada; Europe

    c. Japan; Canada

    d. Canada; the United States ✓

5. Children learn saving and spending habits from which
    of the following?

    a. Parents and grandparents ✓

    b. Math classes

    c. Siblings and friends

    ✓ d. All of the above

6. How are budgeting and money management skills
    normally learned?

    ✓ a. In economics class

    b. By trial and error ✓

    c. From parents

    d. All of the above

    e. None of the above

7. At what age should children begin to learn about money management and the importance of savings accounts?

    a. Sixteen years old because that's when you start driving

    b. After high school graduation so you can handle money at college

√ c. You're never too young to learn about the basics of money management.

    d. All of the above √

8. Money in your savings account is primarily meant to pay for:

    a. Fun stuff that I/we want

    b. Investments to make more money

    c. Specific goals (college) or large purchases (car)

    d. a and b

√ e. b and c √

9. You should pay your bills first and then see what is left over to save.

√ a. True

    b. False √

10. How can you best *begin* making investments?

    a. Use part of your bill money.

    b. Borrow money to invest.

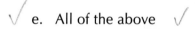 c. Use money from a savings account. ✓

11. Why is it important to learn money management skills early in life?

    a. So you are prepared to take care of yourself when you get older

    b. So you can live a life that is free of money worries

    c. So you are more prepared for being successful

    d. So you can choose what you want to do with your life and not be worried about having enough money

✓ e. All of the above ✓

12. Why is it important to set goals?

    a. It's fun.

    b. It gives you direction.

    c. Successful people do it.

    d. All of the above ✓

✓ e. b and c

13. How can reading this book help you and your family?

    a. It's a good way to develop family togetherness.

    b. It teaches families the skills for success.

    c. Money management is not part of our school's curriculum, so we have to take responsibility to ✓ teach/learn together.

  ✓ d. All of the above

14. People are:

    a. Born rich ✓

    b. Become rich ✓

    c. Rich only if they inherit money

    d. Hard workers if they become rich

    e. Smart workers if they become rich ✓

    f. Rich only if their parents are/were rich

  ✓ g. Rich if they create a mind-set of being rich ✓

Turn to the answer key in Appendix B, p. 217

CHAPTER 1

DOUG'S STORY, OR HOW I BECAME A MILLIONAIRE BY AGE TWENTY-EIGHT

I've learned a lot about money during the past seventy years, much of it through experience. My story starts when I was six years old. My family lived on a small farm in rural Ontario. If you've ever watched episodes of *Little House on the Prairie* or *Anne of Green Gables*, you understand that my generation has made a rather large leap in regard to technical changes. I grew up with horses and wagons, and I certainly don't use them anymore! I've gone from no electricity in my home to the complete opposite. So be easy on my generation; we've seen more and had to change more than any other generation that came before us.

My Irish father grew fruits and vegetables that we often sold at a farmers market in Toronto. Our house was a small bungalow—two bedrooms, a kitchen, living room, and basement. Like most siblings at that time, my twin brother and I slept in the same bed. A wood-and-coal-burning kitchen stove provided the only heat in the house. My mother also cooked all our meals on that stove during the fall, winter, and spring.

During the summer, she cooked on a coal oil stove. We had no running water, no indoor bathroom, and no electricity. You could say that my life has changed in seventy years! But more about that later.

Sometimes on Sunday nights, my parents would invite my aunts, uncles, and cousins for dinner. Afterward, the adults would discuss family matters and the way the world was going. My brother and I were put to bed, and as we went to sleep, sometimes we could hear the adults' conversation. They said that my twin brother, Gerry, was smart, but not very strong. He was considered weakly and got sick often. Then I heard them say that I was not as smart, but strong and healthy. I usually did the harder jobs around the farm. Unfortunately, they labeled and characterized us—not to hurt us or put us down—but it was just the way my family saw us. Maybe this happened to you, too.

What they said became my truth, my identity. I believed what they said about me until I decided to make a change for myself.

Gerry and I shared the farm chores, which were sometimes boring and almost always dirty. Our chores included feeding the pigs, horses, cows, and chickens. We were also expected to keep the pens and areas where the livestock lived clean on a daily basis. I had to do the more demanding jobs and was resentful. I always grumbled to myself that Gerry got it easy.

During the summer holidays, we helped plant, weed, water, and harvest the crops. At the end of the week, Gerry always went with my father to the market in Toronto. I rarely got to go. They took fruit, vegetables, and we had to kill, pluck, and clean the chickens. I didn't like that very much. Every Saturday I helped load the produce for market and watched as Gerry and my father drove away. I was left behind to clean out the pigpens, chicken coops, and any other bull-work that was needed. My resentment grew as I worked. I knew I was the stronger one, but I felt that this arrangement was unfair.

Our family had a fruit and vegetable stand by the road. To make matters worse, it was Gerry's job to sell whatever we had picked that day to people passing by. To me, it looked like a fun and easy job. All he did was sit in the shade and talk to people as they passed. I had to pick berries in the hot sun all day, bent over in the muck in the fields. I wanted to be a part of his world. I kept thinking how unfair it felt to have Gerry sit at the stand during the week and go to Toronto on Saturdays to the market with our father.

Back in those days we didn't have any type of refrigeration, so everything had to be sold quickly. We couldn't keep berries long or they would spoil, and we would lose that income. So I had to keep picking as we sold berries. My mother made jam with the leftover good fruit. The rest would be thrown away. We sold a pint of berries for 10 cents. Haven't prices changed? Now they would sell for about $4. Our family depended on the produce sales. We were sustenance farmers, and the money paid for fuel, clothing, and food, which is how most of the world's farmers live today. There was rarely any money left over for saving or spending on fun things that would make our hearts sing.

One day during the summer of 1939—raspberry-picking time—I persuaded my older brother, Jim, to talk to my father about letting me help sell our berries at the roadside stand. Gerry and I were eight years old at the time.

Reluctantly, my father agreed, but he made it clear that I had to be careful to make the correct change. I was excited at the chance to work the stand. However, while I was getting the berry stand set up the next morning, all kinds of negative thoughts popped into my head.

"I'm dumb."

"I don't know how to make change if someone gives me money."

"I'm scared."

"What if I fail?"

"What if Dad gets angry at me?"

These are the exact same statements that stayed with me into my adult years. That's powerful negative conditioning. We'll talk about positive conditioning later in this book.

Back to the berries …

I had spotted a crate of berries that was left over from the day before. To give you an idea of how much fruit was left, these crates held thirty-six pints of berries. At 10 cents per pint, a whole crate was worth $3.60. My brother hadn't sold the last crate from the previous day, and the berries would be going into my mother's jam recipe soon if they weren't sold. Wow, $3.60 was a lot of money! By today's standards and with inflation, that crate of berries was worth more than $100!

So there I sat at the berry stand. I was all alone. My mind was electric with fear and anticipation. What if ... what if ... what if ...

After a while, a big black car stopped, and a tall man wearing glasses got out of the car with his wife. My greatest hopes and fears were coming true at the same time.

"How much for three pints?" he asked me.

"Ten cents each, sir."

I wasn't very good at math and wasn't supposed to make change. I was embarrassed and didn't want the man to know I couldn't do math. In my state of excitement, I virtually shouted, "Why don't you buy the whole crate, sir?"

The man, perhaps surprised at my directness, asked, "How much?"

"Three dollars," I said.

The man said he would discuss it with his wife; after all, in those days, she would be the one stuck with making the jam from all the berries her husband was about to buy.

After a moment, the tall, lanky man came back and said in a loud voice, "It's a deal." He handed me three $1 bills, and my career was begun!

I sold out of berries in fifteen minutes and didn't have to make change. What a relief. I went back to the fields where Dad was picking more berries. I started working alongside him.

"Doug, what are you doing here?" he said. "You're supposed to be selling at the stand."

I replied with great pride, "I sold the whole crate for $3 to a gentleman and his wife."

After that, my dad didn't question me again about making change or about anything else he thought I couldn't do. I'd sold all the berries in a short amount of time, and we didn't have to throw any of them away. Our relationship and his opinion of me had changed because of that experience. Just think—I created my own self-confidence, somewhat out of desperation, but also to prove that what my family thought about me was not the truth. I was smart. I could sell. I was creative.

This was the first time I really believed in myself. It gave me the courage to accomplish things later in life that I might not have tried otherwise. Now I look back on different occasions in my life when I've achieved my goals and feel good about myself and my capabilities.

So if you have a dream you want to achieve—big or small—take action and do it. Although your mind will play your negative conditioning over and over (and over and over) again, you can still take action. Negative thoughts limit most people in the world—why do you want to fit into this category? Focus on what you want and do it! I did, and I still do. Writing this book is a perfect example of doing something that others may not have thought I could do. Heck, if I'd listened to all the people who said, "He has only an ninth-grade education!" "He didn't go to school!" "He's practically illiterate!" "He's the dumb twin!" then I wouldn't have done anything in my life. It's much more fun not to listen to naysayers and your mind's negative voice. The reward of *not* listening is to live a life of action and success.

SCHOOL DAYS

As boys, my brother and I went to a two-room schoolhouse. We walked a mile to and from school, no matter what the weather. Our teacher was a delightful woman. Myrtle Hammil taught first through fourth grades in one room, while the older children were taught in the other room. It amazes me when I think back on those days and wonder how she could teach four grade levels in the same room and manage all of us so well.

In days gone by, kids had to conform to the school system in even greater ways than they do today. For example, I am naturally left-handed, but when we were learning to write at school, I wasn't allowed to use my left hand. Left-handed kids were thought to be the "devil's children." They forced me to use my right hand. My mind got really mixed up—it was difficult to change how my hands worked and how they connected to my intellect. For me, this was one more challenge that I had to endure but my brother didn't.

One day in third grade, our teacher asked us each to bring 25 cents to school the next day. She took us to a local bank to open savings accounts with our own 25 cent deposit. Ms. Hammil wanted us to learn about the importance of saving money. She taught us that it was important to make regular deposits in the account so we could make interest on the money. She also explained that the bank would pay us interest on our deposits at a certain percentage rate.

I paid attention to the lesson. Learning how to save money and then continuing the habit is a basic lesson that everyone needs to learn at a young age. This is one of the central messages in this book: create a habit of saving that will become a part of you. I explain more about this later in this book.

I went through the eighth grade still in the shadow of my smarter brother, Gerry. He always sat near the front of the room, whereas I took a seat near the back of the class. I'm not sure why; I guess I didn't want to compete with him. During our eighth-grade year, we both became ill with scarlet fever. Gerry ended up with rheumatic fever, causing him to miss that year of school. Because of his illness, he had to repeat eighth grade. I went into ninth grade at the high school that fall without my twin brother.

I didn't do very well in ninth grade. I failed French, English, and math. That meant I had to take grade nine over the following year, and by that time, Gerry had caught up with me. However, the school put me in a different class than Gerry that year. After spending two years in ninth grade, I passed to the tenth grade. At that level, students could choose some of their courses. I wanted to take what they called a "commercial course," which meant I would learn to type. I also liked art and was pretty good at it. So I chose to take a commercial class and an art class. The high school principal, however, insisted that I take French and Latin. He said my hands and fingers were too large to take a typing class.

At the time, I knew that I wouldn't be going to university and that the principal knew that there was no way I could make the grades in French and Latin. After two days in tenth grade, I decided to sell all of the books I had purchased. Then I quit school.

I had spent two years in ninth grade and two days in tenth grade.

My negative thinking patterns were strong and were spurred on by my anger:

"I'm dumb."

"I can't do it."

"I don't want to do it."

"Nobody wants me."

You may be wondering why I'm telling you this story. Of course, you don't want a lesson related to dropping out of school and becoming a millionaire! That's not the kind of lesson I wanted to share with my four kids either.

What I want to share with you is my belief that there is always a way to succeed. If you have a passion and a dream to do something that you believe in, then do it. Don't let anything or anyone stop you from achieving your goal.

So I dropped out and went to work educating myself. I learned what I was good at—what my competencies were—and focused on these areas. I became proficient at carpentry and apprenticed under a master carpenter. I improved my work ethic—sometimes with really strong lessons from my mentors—and educated myself on where my work could be put to best use for the most reward. I've been educating myself ever since and believe it is a lifetime quest. I'll be learning new things until the day I graduate from this great planet I live on.

MY FATHER'S HOUSE

Now that I was not in school full time, my parents wanted me to build a house with indoor plumbing for them. It was a great opportunity for a seventeen-year-old, but I had to build it for free. Guess what? I did it for free. Then my older brother, who was several years older than I and married, wanted a house built. Of course, he also wanted me to design and build the house without pay because he was family. Guess what? I did it for free again. The best thing about building the houses for free was that the experiences gave me practical skills and credibility.

Incidentally, in 1948 the two houses cost $8,000 in materials and subtrades to build. Both of them are still standing today and are valued at more than $500,000 apiece!

MS. HAMMIL'S LESSON

I never forgot Ms. Hammil's basic lesson about saving money. That lesson stayed with me, even during the years that I was serving my apprenticeship as a carpenter.

I spent four years as an apprentice carpenter, and during that time, I worked some extra jobs on the side. I saved $5,000. After receiving my carpenter's papers, I decided to quit my job and go into business for myself as a builder. I purchased three residential lots and decided to build houses on two of the lots. However, before I could build them, I had to have blueprints drawn up.

I found a financial company that would give me a mortgage on the property. It was set up so I could receive progress draws on the mortgage as the buildings were constructed and then completed. The mortgage covered the cost of the building, plus a credit amount that I received from the bank. Of course, I had to have some equity of my own to make the project work. I was able to sell the first two houses before I had finished building them. I made a profit on the sales and began work on the third house. I completed the third house and sold it. This type of building and selling is called "building on spec." In other words, you build the house on speculation and hope to sell it as soon as possible.

MOVING TO TOWN

In the 1960s, farmers were selling their land to developers. I had the feeling that these folks wanted to stay in the community where they had lived all their lives. That was when I decided there was a need for an apartment building. Over a fifteen-year period, I built approximately five hundred houses, a fifty-unit apartment building, and a one hundred-unit apartment building, as well as some industrial and commercial buildings. I thought creatively about a market (the farmers) and their demand (their need to get closer to town) and the supply (my apartments). It was a win-win situation for everyone.

Early in my building career, I occasionally had to appear before our local community planning board. The board consisted of a chairperson and four members. In a small community, people get to know each other. After several appearances before the planning board, we were all familiar with each other.

Mr. Shantz, the chairperson, phoned me one day after a meeting. He invited me to visit with him and his wife at their home the following Saturday. I went on Saturday morning and had coffee and snacks with them. During that meeting, Mr. Shantz shared some of his life story with me. He was a retired executive from the Canadian Pacific Railway where he had worked for many years. About five years before his retirement, he was diagnosed with terminal cancer. He had originally been told that he had six months to a year to live. Mr. Shantz had always wanted a house away from the city. He said he had looked for homes in the country and in small villages in the Toronto area. They purchased the home so that after his passing his wife would enjoy being within walking distance of friends, shopping, and church. The small, white frame house, with a yard enclosed on the front and sides with a picket fence, was just what the doctor ordered, you might say.

Mr. Shantz gave me a tour of the house and property after we finished our coffee. The house was near the main street of Markham. I thought his property consisted of the thirty-foot-wide and almost two-hundred-fifty-foot-deep lot. However, at the rear of that space was the surprise of my life: about three acres of land spread out like a mini golf course. A ravine with a meandering brook separated the two areas of the property. It was beautiful and had majestic hundred-year-old trees. The grass was manicured. I fell in love with the property, which was located right in the heart of the village. What a find!

I immediately asked Mr. Shantz if he ever decided to sell, would he give me the first opportunity to purchase it? He said he would. We sealed the agreement with a handshake, and I left his home as excited as if I'd won a lottery. Over the next year or so, my heart and my focus were dedicated to owning that property. Then, to my delight and surprise, Mr. Shantz invited me to join him on his property. I went, and we took a walk toward the ravine. When we stopped, he said to me, "I think you could build fifty suites on this site. Do you want to purchase it? I'm ready to sell."

"Of course," I said. "How much?"

"Twenty-five thousand dollars," he said.

"It's a deal," I said, and we shook hands.

I went to my lawyer and formalized an offer to purchase the property with $2,000 down and the balance of $23,000 due in eighteen months.

Then I showed the property to my designer, Jack Shaw, whom I had worked with on all of my houses, and asked if he would design the fifty-unit apartment building. He agreed to take on the project. Jack also asked if I wanted a partner. We became fifty-fifty partners. His job was to design the building; I was to construct it. Jack was a very talented and creative designer, even though he wasn't actually an architect. He had relationships with certified engineers and architects who could certify his work.

After Jack and I had spent about a year planning the project, getting our financing in place, and securing approvals from local authorities, we were ready to start building. While getting ready to build the fifty-unit apartment building, Mr. Shantz shared his plans with me to build a new house—his dream home. He asked my advice on what to build and how much it would cost for me to build it for him. At the time, Mr. Shantz was seventy-five years old. I admired him for thinking the way he did. But he wanted to build the home on his lot, and I had already fallen in love with the entire property. I gently persuaded him to sell it to me and offered him an alternative to building the dream home. Instead, after I built an apartment on the lot, he would have first choice of all the suites and could rent whichever one he pleased. We concluded the deal, and Mr. and Mrs. Shantz moved into a beautiful, two-bedroom apartment.

Mr. Shantz loved living in the apartment with the view over the valley and Rouge River. This was really more suited to his lifestyle. After living in the apartment for some time, Mr. Shantz decided to stay, and he sold his remaining land to me. I built my own dream home on the property.

My wife and I have lived in this lovely home for forty years, and Mr. Shantz and his wife lived out their days on the land he loved.

THE BEST LAID PLANS ...

In hindsight, I'm amazed that I took on such a huge project. Remember, I'd only built a few houses, and here I was buying a massive piece of property in the downtown centre and developing one of the largest residential projects the town had ever seen!

While building the apartments, everything was going well until we got to the "brown coat" of the plastering. Today we would use drywall to enclose the rooms. In those days, we used plaster, a brown or rough coat first. Then we applied the final coat, which was a smooth, white finish that could be painted or wallpapered. During the plastering process one day, Jack came into my office with a surprise for me. Not only was Jack a designer, but he was also a perfectionist. He couldn't stand the imperfection of the plastering and wanted out of the deal. He wanted the $25,000 capital money he had invested, plus another $25,000 for the work he had done, for a total of $50,000. I tried to talk him out of it, but to no avail. He refused to change his mind. He told me if I didn't buy him out, he would sell his share to someone else. Because I didn't have the money to pay him off, I wasn't sure what to do. I had never had any experience with this sort of challenge before. Did that old negative conditioning come back? Of course!

"I don't know if I can do it."

"What if I fail?"

"What if I go broke?"

"No one wants to be my partner."

I decided to see my lawyer and get some advice. Three or four days later, I went to the mortgage company that held the mortgage on the property for the apartment complex. I told them exactly what I needed to buy out Jack. I requested that the company add the $50,000 on to the $600,000 mortgage that it already had encumbered the property with, which would allow me to buy out my partner. The mortgage company approved the extra $50,000 on the mortgage, and I bought out Jack. I became sole owner of the apartment building.

HOW I BECAME A MILLIONAIRE AT TWENTY-EIGHT

About six months after I had bought out my partner's share of the apartment building, all fifty suites were rented. There were zero vacancies, and for those of you who know real estate, you understand how great that is. Furthermore, the value of the building was worth considerably more than it was worth when I purchased my partner's share. And I was only twenty-eight.

When I was able to raise the mortgage from $600,000 to $650,000 and buy out my partner with that mortgage money, I leveraged my position (or ownership) from 50 percent to 100 percent. When I had the building 100 percent rented, I leveraged the value from $650,000 to $2 million. If I had sold the building and paid my taxes, my net proceeds would have been more than $1 million, thus arriving at the millionaire status. I was a millionaire at age twenty-eight![1]

It was one of the best deals I ever made, and it was all because my partner wanted out of the deal. Why was it a good deal? Because we have remained friends, and he still designed the houses I built. It was a win-win situation for everyone. Being rich isn't about taking something from someone else. Being rich is about having rich and rewarding relationships, which is what I had with Jack.

I was able to turn this obstacle into an opportunity. Honesty and integrity were first and foremost during our partnership. I also maintained that integrity with the mortgage company. Treat everyone like you want to be treated, and it will pay dividends in the short and long term.

PAY YOURSELF WHEN?

When I was a sixteen years old, I read a book called *The Richest Man in Babylon* by George S. Clason. I learned about the Babylon Theory—pay yourself first at least 10 percent of the money you receive before paying anyone else. By using this formula, you learn to live on 90 percent of your money. Psychologically your brain tells you that the 90 percent you have to pay your bills and living costs is actually 100 percent. After you start doing this, you'll never miss the 10 percent that you put into your savings account.

---

1   I didn't sell the building at that time, though, and netted much more than $1 million when I sold the building more than twenty-five years later.

After you have saved a certain amount, invest it into a growth or interest-bearing investment and never spend it. You will put your money to work for more and more money. The greatest thing about savings and investments is that they work twenty-four hours a day, seven days a week.

As an employee, a regular workweek is five days or forty hours. Think about five days you work compared to the seven days your invested money works. That means your money works 104 more days a year than you do. When you continue to work the numbers, during the fifty years between age fifteen and age sixty-five, your money will work 5,200 days more than you do. Isn't that a great kind of partnership to have?

Now look at it a little differently. If you were to borrow money for a car payment or mortgage, you have to pay interest on the loan. It costs you 104 days a year that money isn't making money for you. Common sense tells us that it's better to invest money and let it work for you than to have the continual cost of borrowed money. You have to earn enough money to pay the loan and interest back or go broke. More on money management later in this book. For now, back to my story …

CHANGING MY PROFESSION

In 1969, I decided to change my career from a builder to a real estate salesperson. After taking many courses in law, economics, and business, I got my real estate license and started working for a real estate broker. I intended to eventually go into business with my own real estate brokerage. However, before I could go into business for myself, I had to complete a two-year interim period as a salesperson. It was like being an apprentice carpenter all over again!

After serving two years, I opened my own offices, Armour Real Estate Inc. I started with two salesmen in 1972.

In the mid-1970s, I purchased a Century 21 franchise. Even though I was trained in industrial commercial leasing and selling investment, my company mainly sold residential property. In 1982, 1983, and 1984, my company was the top producing company in the Century 21 system in all of Canada! My team was fantastic, and we achieved great success together!

In 1994, I decided to sell my real estate company. I had about seventy-five agents at the time. Having done well as a broker and in the real estate agency business, I had the opportunity to sell my company to one of my top agents, Jenny Cook, and her husband. Being in business for yourself gives you the opportunity to expand your dreams the way you want to; whereas when you work for another firm or corporation, there are limits to what you can do. Why? Because you are an employee, not the boss.

After getting out of the real estate business, a local ski resort came up for sale. My family and I had been members of the club since 1969, so when the opportunity presented itself, I bought the club with the aim of turning it into a four-season resort. I just loved this place—the nature, the feelings, the sport. It was a project of love.

The club was rundown and needed to be modernized for the twenty-first century. With my experience in carpentry, building, development, and the real estate business, I had useful skills going into a business that I knew very little about. The courses I had taken also benefited me in this adventure. Most businesses have certain things in common and similar requirements to operate successfully and make a profit. These requirements include a vision statement, mission statement, marketing strategy, business plan, and enough capital for expansion. The list goes on and on.

I had hoped over time to develop a golf course on the resort site, as well as build approximately fifty houses around the property. However, the Ontario government passed legislation preventing any new development on all lands east, north, and west of Toronto. This area is called the Oak Ridge Moraine and is the home of a large underground water source that feeds Lake Ontario to the south and Lake Simcoe to the north. All this land is frozen for development.

My two hundred-fifty-acre ski resort was on the highest elevation of the Oak Ridge Moraine. Because I couldn't develop it, the resort was dependent strictly on skiing three or four months out of the year for its revenue. Nevertheless, using creativity, we rented the grand lodge for weddings from spring until late fall. What a beautiful place for a wedding!

SELLING WHAT YOU LOVE

After owning and managing the club for eleven years, I had an opportunity to sell the ski club. I received my asking price, which covered the money I had put into the resort and the improvements I had made during my tenure as owner. Because I wasn't able to develop the land any further, and with the very real problem of shorter and shorter winters, I know I did the right thing in selling. I had initially bought the club because I loved it; I had so many happy family memories wrapped up in that place that it seemed the natural thing to do at the time.

I came to learn that emotions can cloud business decisions. It was wise to sell and move on to other investment projects. My daughter Sarah, who equally loved the ski club, always reminded me that I had bought into the service industry, not the real estate industry. I never liked the service industry, even though I continue to love land development projects. I've learned never to get attached to something. There is always another door of opportunity to open.

LIFELONG LEARNING

Over the years, I took many courses, including public speaking, economics, real estate appraisal, law, business, and personal development. These classes provided some of the tools that helped me succeed in business. I know that part of my success is due to persistence, self-confidence, and surrounding myself with the right people.

Now that you know a bit more about how I became a richer me, we can now turn to giving you the knowledge and skills to become a richer you.

FAMILY SUCCESS CHECKLIST

$ You have negative conditioning. It is your *job* not to believe it.

$ You can create positive conditioning. This book will help you.

$ Open a savings account.

$ Pay yourself first. Save 10 percent of all you earn or receive.

$ Riches are more than money. Riches are the sum of your relationships, too.

$ Live with integrity. Do what you say, and say what you do.

$ Formal education is great. However, there are other ways to learn, too. Find out what they are and strengthen your existing competencies.

PART I

HOW TO BECOME A RICHER YOU

QUESTIONNAIRE: WHAT IS RICH?

INSTRUCTIONS

Complete the list of questions in the space provided.

1. When someone is called "rich," how much money do you think they have?

2. What other types of riches or wealth are there besides money?

3. When will you know that you are rich?

Doug Meharg built and designed his first home, a home for his family, at the age of 17.

Another perspective of the first home Doug built.

CHAPTER 2

CREATING A SELF-IMAGE

"Whatever qualities the rich may have, they can be acquired by anyone with the tenacity to become rich. The key, I think, is confidence. Confidence and an unshakable belief it can be done and that you are the one to do it."

–FELIX DENNIS, *HOW TO GET RICH*

Who we are and how much success we enjoy begins with how we see ourselves, not how others see us.

As you read in Chapter One, I created my own self-confidence by overcoming my fear and embracing new opportunities. My healthy sense of confidence was directly related to my ability to become rich. In this chapter, I reveal some ways that you can create your own healthy and positive self-image, as well as help your children to do so.

First, let's look at how your self-image develops and what you can do to improve yours.

NEGATIVE LANGUAGE

How we see ourselves and what we think we can accomplish is tied to what we've been told and what we've experienced from the time we were kids. If you are a parent, then this is a double lesson for you. Think about the things that were said about you, positive and negative, when you were a child. You probably still hear many of them in your mind today. They affect your decisions, your attitudes, and your successes— or lack thereof.

Most people hear negative comments about themselves in their minds most of the time: *I'm stupid. I'm fat. I'm broke. I'm alone. No one loves me.* The list goes on. We wouldn't say these things to our friends, yet we let our minds say these things to ourselves. People come to believe this negativity like it's the truth. Yet, what people hear in their minds is often what they heard others say about them when they were kids, just like when my parents commented about my brother Gerry and me.

Some people, like myself, have decided to take things into their own hands and change the comments from negative to positive. This creates a healthy self-image.

When a child hears only negative feedback, that is what the child most likely believes about himself. Unfortunately, most people naturally gravitate to the negative statements they hear and believe them. The negative words become embedded in our subconscious and then grow into our beliefs about ourselves.

You know the kinds of statements I'm talking about: *You'll never amount to anything. You aren't smart enough to become wealthy. You're not as smart as your sister. You can't do that. You'll never …*

These statements are someone else's opinion of you, not your opinion of you! You can reject those statements. They're not true. If you allow them to influence how you feel about yourself, you let yourself be less than you can be. All of the potential you'll ever need is already inside of you. When someone says something negative about you, don't believe it as the truth. Perhaps thank them for sharing and then move on. This is a great skill to teach our kids.

PRAISING YOUR CHILDREN

To build healthy and positive images in your children is to reward and encourage them every day. Praise them whenever possible. A friend of mine shared with me that when her children were small, she tried to find a positive thing to tell them every night at bedtime. It could be as simple as, "You did a great job getting ready for bed tonight." Compliment them on progress, things well done, and good attitudes. Let them know you are proud of them and they are of value to you, not only in the words you say, but in the way you treat them.

How a person feels about himself has an impact on how successful he is as an adult and how wealthy he becomes. To become a richer you, you must work on your negative mind chatter first (that's what I call that voice inside our heads that says such negative things). Then you need to be aware of how you influence your children's mind chatter when you verbalize negative comments within their hearing.

BACK TO THE FARM

In Chapter One, I told you about my childhood. What I heard my parents and relatives saying about me made a strong impression on how I thought of myself. It affected my attitude and how well I did in school.

I knew my parents always thought my twin was smarter than I. I knew I was expected to do the hard work with my dad and older brother because I had physical strength. All those Saturdays that I saw my twin brother get into the truck and go into town to the farmers market with our dad left me feeling taken for granted, and I didn't feel like I would ever make very much of myself. I felt like my own parents and family thought I was only good at labor. But I didn't want to be satisfied with that. I wanted to *be* someone and to live a better life than I had as a child.

After many years of living without electricity, my mother decided she was going to take action and arrange to get electric service for our home. She was exhausted from working so hard on the farm and in the house, and she wanted just one thing for herself and her family—electric lights! My dad didn't spend his money on what he considered frivolity, and of course, lights were frivolous. Knowing that my father wouldn't approve, Mom arranged for the electrical contractor to come out to the house while my dad was away for ten days.

As scheduled, the workers came. In addition to putting electrical lights and connections in the house, my mother had them put a light in the barn for my dad to work by when it got dark. This would be especially nice during the winter months with short days and long nights.

When my dad came back to the farm, he arrived home to a house lit up like a ballpark stadium in the dark country landscape! We had turned on every single light in the house to surprise him. Because my parents didn't always get along, I expected my dad to explode at Mom. However, to my surprise, he didn't say much to her about it after he found out that she had put a light in the barn for him.

It was the first time I remember my mother ever standing up to him and doing what she wanted for herself and the family. Her actions made a huge impression on me. She rose above her circumstances and made a choice to make them better. I've always remembered that about Mom. It was clear at that moment that she had ignored her negative mind chatter and had acted in spite of her fear. She had embraced a new opportunity, and it changed her life forever. In fact, it changed our family's life forever.

When you overcome the negative thoughts that play over and over in your mind, you can move on to become anything you choose to be. You can be successful, wealthy, and satisfied in life. And live in the light, not in darkness!

SHARING YOUR POTENTIAL

Take every opportunity you have to teach your children that they are valuable to themselves and to society. They have specific gifts and talents that no one else has. Others may be similar, but each person is a distinct individual. Each child is filled with potential and should be taught that they are unique and special. They don't have to settle for being something that someone else labels them.

I worked hard during my young years on the farm and building houses. I knew I wanted more and kept focusing on what the next step would be. I believed that I could accomplish what I wanted and didn't let anything stop me. Yes, I had some obstacles and challenges, but they didn't stop me. Most of the time I made them into opportunities, and I strongly believe that regardless of the circumstances and changes with time, you can too.

THE SIX MENTAL FACULTIES

It is important for you to understand how your mind works before we go further in learning about how to be successful and be a good money manager and live an abundant life.

Most people have heard of right-brain and left-brain thinking. Simply stated, the right brain is the more creative, visual, and intuitive side, and the left brain is the more fact-oriented and analytical side. I want to focus on the six mental faculties and how they work together. By learning this, you will be better able to apply the lessons in this book to your everyday life. You'll know how your brain works and how to put it to better use.

* **Perception** is the ability to be aware of what's going on around you. It also provides insight. You experience situations and learn from them. Your perception is closely related to your physical senses—sight, hearing, touch, smell, and taste. This faculty gives you a mental understanding, awareness, and comprehension of things around you.

* **Reasoning** is your ability to think things through and make assumptions or decisions. Your mind takes all the information it

has about a situation, including facts learned, and processes them to come up with a conclusion. It's how we form judgments about things and people.

* **Memory** is like a file cabinet. It's where your brain keeps all the information that you gather through your senses. What you learn and what you experience is logged in your memory and can be used if you choose to recall information. Some people say their memory is better than others', but all of us have the same basic ability. We keep our life lessons available so we don't continue to make the same mistakes.

* **Intuition** is an ability that everyone has. It is experienced as a feeling. This faculty is the ability to know or learn something without consciously using reasoning. You don't always understand it immediately.

* **Will** is sometimes called *will power*. This mental faculty is the power of making a decision and then exercising control over yourself to accomplish a goal. It is characterized by persistence, perseverance, and determination. You may experience it as strong-mindedness and intense focus.

* **Imagination** is the faculty that enables you to create mental images of something that may not be present or has not yet happened. Our imaginations and dreams are referred to as our "metaphysical reality." It is separate from our physical and material world, but just as important to the mind. This is the faculty that works with visualization and is also the area of creativity. Inventions and new ideas are born here.

UNDERSTANDING SELF-IMAGE AND CONFIDENCE

We are all taught in school about our physical senses, but we don't always have an awareness of the six mental faculties. They are available to us to tap into and use every day. The first step to using them is becoming aware. The preceding section provided you with the definitions, and in the rest of this book, you can apply some of the faculties to gaining a better understanding of how to become a richer you.

You have a conscious mind and a subconscious mind. The information you take in through your conscious mind is logged in your subconscious. Those negative statements you heard when you were young are recorded there, but you can keep them or replace them with more positive sentences or thoughts when they surface into your consciousness. It's your choice. Don't allow yourself to dwell on negative thoughts. Make the effort to be aware of your thoughts.

WHY YOUR PARADIGM MATTERS

One factor that most people overlook in developing their self-image is their paradigm. A paradigm is the lens through which you view your world. Each of us has a set of lenses that is created from our culture, conditioning, beliefs, assumptions, principles, values, and practices. These influence how you see things and what you take from your experiences. With study, you can become aware of your paradigms and change them if you want to. Because we all have paradigms, wouldn't it make sense to shift our paradigms to positive, abundant ones rather than negative, self-limiting ones? I think so, too.

The term "paradigm" has become more common over the past ten years or so in business, personal, and professional development. I'm sure you've participated in a conversation or overheard one in which people were discussing a paradigm shift in how they think, live, or work.

An interesting side note about this term is that it isn't as modern or as new as we might think. It is actually a very old term. The word "paradigm" appeared as early as the fifteenth century in English. The original meaning was "an example or pattern." That hasn't really changed over the past four hundred years. During the 1960s, people started using paradigm in science as a reference to a theoretical framework. Most of us use the word to mean the prevalent viewpoint of things. We use the term much more broadly in our current society. For our purposes, it refers to change in how you think and the way you live.

Changing how you look at yourself is the first step in creating a new paradigm.

Some paradigms are more common than others, and some are more useful than others. The one you are creating regarding your ability to make money is one that I believe is more useful. This book suggests that you can become a richer you—and this is a clear paradigm shift away from where you might be.

By reading this book and working through the activities, your thought process will move away from one that may be stuck in thinking about what you don't have and what you wish you had. You might be looking at someone else's life and wondering why they have so much and are doing more than you. Your new paradigm is going to be one of progress and looking forward to using your new way of thinking and your new skills to become a richer you.

You may be reading this book to discover what rich people know that you may not. However, consider that some people who are wealthy don't necessarily have a positive mind-set or a good self-image. That is one of the reasons people lose their fortunes.

If you have what I refer to as "faulty wiring"—a poor self-image and lack of confidence—it can greatly limit your success. With faulty wiring, you can have all the knowledge and practical money skills, but you'll rarely sustain success over the long run, despite having a large bank account. Living in negativity takes its toll on everything you do, whether you start out rich or poor. Success begins with you and the paradigm you choose to create for yourself and your family.

Why not chose to shift your paradigm toward a positive self-image and high level of confidence? This will create good wiring, and you will have the foundation to move on to the next stage of becoming a richer you.

FAMILY SUCCESS CHECKLIST

$ How we see ourselves and what we think we can accomplish is tied to what we've been told and what we've experienced.

$ Who we are and how much success we enjoy begins with how we see ourselves.

$ Your thoughts become attitudes that are reflected in behaviour and, ultimately, results.

$ Negative statements are someone else's opinion of you. They're not the truth. You can reject their statements.

$ A parenting skill that is important for building a healthy and positive image in our kids is to reward and encourage them. Praise them whenever possible.

$ Every child is filled with potential and should be taught that they are unique, talented, and special. They don't have to settle for being something that someone else labels them.

$ Remember the six mental faculties to make a prosperous life—perception, reasoning, memory, intuition, will, and imagination. They are as important as our physical senses—touch, taste, smell, sound, and sight. Use the mental faculties and physical senses in all of your visualizations.

Doug Meharg was 18 when he built a house for his older brother.

Doug built and designed his second home one year after building his first.

CHAPTER 3

FOCUS ON SUCCESS

"The longer I live, the more I realize the impact of attitude on life. Attitude, to me, is more important than facts. It is more important than the past, the education, the money, than circumstances, than failure, than successes, than what other people think or say or do. It is more important than appearance, giftedness, or skill. It will make or break a company ... a church ... a home. The remarkable thing is we have a choice every day regarding the attitude we will embrace for that day. We cannot change our past ... we cannot change the fact that people will act in a certain way. The only thing we can do is play on the one string we have, and that is our attitude. I am convinced that life is 10 percent what happens to me and 90 percent of how I react to it. And so it is with you ... we are in charge of our attitudes."

—CHARLES R. SWINDOLL

Your self-image, your attitude, and focusing on what you want are three factors that influence your results. All the money in the world can't change a low self-esteem, a bad attitude, or focusing on what you *don't* want (debt, illness, unhappiness). However, a healthy, positive self-image, a positive attitude, and focusing on what you do want can overcome any obstacles and conquer most challenges. These three things are the foundation to my formula for success.

You are completely in charge of your own attitude. No one can make you feel anything that you don't allow or choose to feel. Just because you're going through a period of challenges doesn't mean you have to have a cranky attitude and take things out on the people around you. When you choose to keep a positive attitude through any circumstance, you can take charge. Instead of feeling like a victim of change, you are the master of change. Your attitude has a huge effect on your ability to succeed in life.

BAD ATTITUDES ARE DISABILITIES

When I first started building houses, I did a lot of the work myself, and I was so tired. In fact, I know now that I was overworking myself to the point of exhaustion and, consequently, was a very sour individual!

One day on a housing project, we were pouring concrete for a basement floor. During the day, I had worked with the concrete workers to set up the floor and ready it for leveling and troweling to create a smooth finish. When 5:00 PM came around on Friday, the other workers were finished with their day and headed home for the weekend. That left me alone to finish up the job. The humidity was really high that day, so the concrete wasn't setting right.

Even though I'd already worked a ten-hour day, I had to stay. I worked alone through the night until 9:00 AM the next day to get the job done correctly.

I was exhausted and ready to go home and get some sleep when a real estate agent and a prospective buyer drove up. Uh-oh. I was so tired I couldn't even see straight! What was I going to do? Why did they have to show up now? Couldn't they see I was busy and had no time for them?

The agent wanted me to show him and his client around the house and property. I reluctantly did what he asked and then left to go home and get the sleep I desperately wanted.

As I departed, I hoped that the agent would write up an offer for the client to purchase the house. On Monday morning I saw the agent at a local restaurant. Because I was now well rested and feeling terrific, I decided to say hello and ask him if the prospective buyer liked the excellent home I was building. To my dismay, his comments were the opposite of what I was expecting.

He put his coffee cup down and barked, "They would not purchase a house from you if hell froze over!"

"Why?" I asked.

"You were rude, ugly, and just miserable," he said.

From that point on, I knew I needed a better attitude. If I had delegated the work on Friday instead of taking it all on myself that night, I might have made a sale. I chose to do it myself and paid a price. I lost that sale because I was overly tired and had a bad attitude because I had elected to work twenty-four hours straight. I could have put on a happy face during the showing if I had wanted to. Instead, I was sour.

Are you walking around being a sourpuss? Are your kids? Why? Figure out what you need to do to be able to put on a smile, even under difficult circumstances, and adopt a good attitude.

Scott Hamilton, an Olympic gold medal figure skater from the United States, once said, "The only disability in life is a bad attitude." This statement can shift your paradigm. If you think positively and maintain a positive attitude, your problems may not go away or solve themselves, but you will be open to the good things your attitude is attracting. In other words, a bad attitude in your daily life causes obstacles between you and your riches. Having a great attitude in your daily life helps you steer around any obstacles that come between you and your riches. Which would you rather have?

WORK ON YOURSELF FIRST

We all know someone in our immediate family who could use a better attitude. But remember, *you must work on yourself first*. You can't give someone else a new attitude, just like you can't change someone else. You have to change yourself from within first and encourage others in their efforts to create a better attitude.

Think about how contagious a smile is. Most of us find it difficult to return a scowl for a smile. When you meet a stranger, it doesn't cost you a thing to give her a smile, and it may brighten her day and give her a reason to feel encouraged. What about people who are always grouchy and hard to get along with? No one makes them that way—they choose it for themselves, daily! People can decide to go through life with a bad attitude or a good attitude. The truth is that the time will pass anyway. Why not spend the time positively and productively?

Kahlil Gibran was a Lebanese-born American philosopher and essayist in the early part of the twentieth century. He once said, "Your living is determined not so much by what life brings to you as by the attitude you bring to life; not so much by what happens to you as by the way your mind looks at what happens." Gibran's observations apply to how you handle challenges or even everyday life. Basically, you attract certain things and situations into your life by your positive or negative thoughts and energy. Many people don't realize that they are the cause of what comes into their lives.

John C. Maxwell's book, *The Winning Attitude,* is a great source of information about developing an attitude that will serve you positively in life. Maxwell talks about someone taking a flight over his new hometown. One of the main things the passenger learned from the pilot was the importance of watching the altitude of the plane in relationship to the ground. It meant the difference between successfully reaching his destination or crashing the plane.

Your attitude is a product of the way you think. You need to learn how to think differently so you can create a better life. When you combine this with money management skills, you will achieve success.

Whatever you choose to do is affected by your attitude. How do you develop a positive attitude or change one from a negative to a positive? There are two kinds of statements:

I can't do …

I can do …

Let's examine these statements. Each is based in beliefs about yourself and your self-image.

First, let's look at the "I can't do" statement. Examples are: *I can't drive a car. I can't pass this class. I can't go to college. I can't save money. I can't change the way I think. I can't change my career. I can't learn new things.* "I can't" statements sound like, "She won't let me," or "Dad will kill me if I don't become a dentist." Every one of these statements is a self-imposed limitation that you place on yourself. We all need to learn to get out of our own way so success will be much easier to grab a hold of.

Negative beliefs set you up for a negative attitude. They keep you from exploring and learning new things and new skills. A negative attitude keeps you inside a box with no way out until you decide to change your attitude and allow yourself to get out and see what's in the world. The world is full of possibilities. Your attitude drives whether you get out of the box to become a richer you.

You can have an "I can" attitude. This attitude opens doors and breaks down walls. Anything is possible. For example: *I can drive a car. I can pass this class. I can go to college. I can save money. I can change the way I think. I can change my career. I can learn new things.* Remember those other statements like, "She won't let me"? Those can be shifted to, "She may understand what I want when I communicate my needs to her," or "I can tell Dad how I feel about becoming a dentist so he will see why I need to become a carpenter."

Before you get too carried away with possibilities, there are a few absolutes in our world that you need to consider. You won't sprout wings on your back and fly around the world. You won't get gills and be able to swim under the sea without air tanks or a submarine. You won't be able to exceed the speed of light in your new sports car in spite of how much you would like to. You can't physically be in two different places at the same time. These may sound silly, but a few things are absolutes— at least in this day and age. Perhaps with scientific and technological advancements we may be flying, breathing in water, transporting between two places, and moving at the speed of light—but not right now.

That aside, you can do many things successfully. The attitude starts with positive statements and beliefs about yourself.

THE POWER OF LANGUAGE

Some people wake up each day and think to themselves,

"What a great day. I'm so glad to be alive and living an abundant life. I have everything I need in my grasp to live successfully."

However, some people wake up each day and think to themselves,

"Here comes another crummy day at work. I hate work. I wish I could call in sick. I hate my boss. I never have anything to wear."

Wow, what a different mind-set these two people have. Every time you say something that begins with *don't, not, never,* and *no* you get more of exactly what you don't want.

We say negative statements all the time without consciously thinking about it. Listen to each other as a family and encourage the use of positive statements for better results. Try these options on for size:

INSTEAD OF	USE
Don't forget …	Remember to …
Don't be late …	I'll see you on time …
Don't drop that …	Hold onto that …
Don't be scared …	Be brave …
Don't spend your money on junk food …	Spend your money on healthy snacks …
Don't waste your time …	Spend your time wisely …
There aren't any monsters …	Only good monsters live here …

I'm sure you can think of many more statements like these based on the ideas of the book *Law of Attraction* by Michael J. Losier on page 25. You'll begin to notice improvements in behaviours, attitudes, self-images, and confidence levels when you make positive statements. Consciously correct yourself until it becomes a habit that replaces the old way of thinking and saying things.

Positive self-image and positive beliefs are the foundation of your positive attitude. They empower you. They enable you to create the better life you want for yourself and your family. You can learn money management skills to become a richer you. You need to first believe that it is possible—*which it is*. Then you need to keep that belief of "I can" and apply it to your everyday thinking: *I can be rich. I can be successful. My family can be successful. My children can be successful.*

Reject the old thinking patterns and negative beliefs and thoughts. They are invalid. You're not under their power anymore. Those old beliefs disempower you. You are beyond that now and can leave it behind. You can overcome those old thoughts and beliefs. You are living a life of enjoyment and are on a journey of discovery, learning, and, ultimately, financial success as a family.

I WON'T!

I've learned over the years that most people who say, "I can't," really mean, "I won't." They would rather give in to their fear of failure or negative beliefs about themselves than step out of their comfort zone and accomplish something new—for themselves and their family. They would rather settle for what they have and complain about it than take a risk and move beyond where they thought they had to stay. "I can't save money and invest," often means, "I don't want to put aside 10 percent of my income and invest it for future money. I'd rather just spend it as I get it." "I can't be wealthy" often means, "I don't want to learn what I need to that would give me the skills I need to be wealthy."

The difference between "I can't" and "I won't" is in your control. It's your decision whether you would rather be stuck in "I can't" and spend your life making excuses. I challenge you to start changing your negative "I can'ts" into positive "I cans."

Some people use the excuse, "I would, but I can't because I don't know how." If you've been thinking and saying, "I can't be wealthy because I don't know how," then you've come to the right place.

I understand that changing from the old habit of "I can't" to a new way of seeing the world through an "I can" attitude is challenging. I've gone through it myself. I've helped others go through the process. I know you can do this and so can your family. It's okay to be afraid of change and the unknown. However, if you want to move forward and create a successful future for your family, it's not okay to use those feelings as excuses. If you want to win, you have to run the race.

GOOD TIMES, BAD TIMES

Have you ever noticed that it's easy to have a good attitude when everything is going the way you want it to go? When things are running smoothly and there's only an occasional speed bump, you can maintain a good attitude without breaking a sweat. The challenge is to maintain a good attitude when things feel like they're falling apart. If you've ever read about the sinking of the Titanic, the stories say that the survivors in the lifeboats could hear people singing as the ship finally broke up and sank into the cold North Atlantic Ocean. After reading this, a friend of mine said to me, "I'm not sure I'd be singing as we went down. It would be more like screaming!"

For us, we can either scream all the way to the bottom, or we can enjoy the rest of the trip. This isn't meant to trivialize the tragedy or the terrible experience that the people on the Titanic went through or the loss experienced by their families. It's meant to make a point that no matter how small or how big your circumstances feel, you still have a choice about what kind of attitude you will keep through the experience. Many people who come out of a terrible tragedy have a survival attitude that no matter what happens, they will get through it.

WHEN THE GOING GETS TOUGH

Although perhaps cliché, the saying "When the going gets tough, the tough get going" is a powerful statement. It's all about attitude and perseverance. Most people want to run when things get too tough to handle or they perceive their circumstances as unbearable. It is amazing that soldiers who survive battles or that people who survived the Holocaust can think positively. *The Diary of Anne Frank* reveals a young girl whose attitude showed amazing resilience under horrific circumstances. She didn't survive the Second World War, but her legacy is an example of maintaining a giving and forgiving attitude, no matter what.

Most of us will never go through an extreme tragedy; however, we often believe that our own circumstances are unbearable. And that may be true at that moment. No one knows what it's like to live in someone else's skin, but it is important that we learn to not only exercise our good attitude in good times, but also through challenging times. It helps us get through those difficult days and encourages others to do the same.

I usually use affirming statements such as "I know I can get through this," or "My positive faith and love will see me through this circumstance," or "Stay peacefully calm; things will pass." These have all helped me in the past, and I will use them for a long time yet. Make up some statements that can help you readjust your attitude when you're faced with difficulties. Do this before you're faced with a bad time so you are prepared. Then, when the going gets tough, you know exactly what to do.

KEEP A RECORD OF SUCCESSES

Over the years, I've learned that one of the best ways to build my confidence is to keep a record of my successes. I have a special notebook to write down my achievements—great and small. That way, if I have any doubts with a new project or goal, I can go back and look at the track record I've built. It gives me evidence that can rid me of any doubts that might come up. Doubts are negative energy that can defeat me if I let them. They can defeat you, too, if you are not prepared to handle them when they come up. Get yourself a notebook and start keeping a record of your successes. This is also a terrific activity to do with your partner and kids.

Realize that there are going to be bumps in the road. There are going to be hills and valleys to cross, but we need to enjoy the journey. Life's challenges are just like that. After you've been through the worst you thought you'd ever see, you will have increased your confidence and can even more successfully employ your "I can" attitude.

Successes need to be celebrated. When someone in your family brings home a success story, throw a party. Treat it like a big thing, because it is.

Encourage your kids to share their successes with you and their siblings. Have them write about their achievements in their record of success. It doesn't have to be a long entry, but be sure to have them keep a record. They can always look back on it and have evidence that proves they are successful in achieving their goals.

PATIENCE, PATIENCE, PATIENCE

It is important to understand that even with a healthy self-image, confidence, and a positive attitude, it may take some time to become a richer you. This is because you are undoing a lot of negative conditioning accumulated over many years. This stuff isn't going to work overnight— but it will work. Be patient.

When I was in primary public school in grade two, our teacher, Myrtle Hammil, showed us how we could create a beautiful green plant from a big thick carrot. Most of the kids at our school came from a farming community and had stored carrots for the winter. Our job was to get a big carrot and cut it in half. We then made a cup from the half we kept. I took my carrot home and hung the part where the root would be upside down from the kitchen ceiling. I had to keep the cup part filled with water.

I waited and waited for something to happen. Nothing happened. It seemed like a dog's age that I waited. Well, lo and behold! One morning I visited my carrot creation on the kitchen table, and new green stems were sprouting! Within weeks, they had spread out around the carrot. The carrot was growing toward the ceiling and provided a beautiful green array of carrot leaves during the winter months.

This little project taught me about patience. It takes time between the sowing and the harvest—or in other words, between the learning, the doing, and the results. I kept watering that upside-down carrot and got wonderful results, but it took some time. Decide to keep watering your carrot!

I encourage you to perform this exercise with your young kids. Enjoy the project and understand how important patience is in building up wealth.

FROM DEPRESSED TO SUCCESS

"Success is not final; failure is not fatal: it is the courage to continue that counts."

–WINSTON CHURCHILL

We've talked a lot about being successful, but just what is success? The Encarta Dictionary defines it as "the achievement of something planned or attempted. It is an impressive achievement, especially the attainment of fame, wealth, or power." Success can also be defined as something that turns out well. Somebody who has significant achievements is considered a success. However, people may have different definitions for what they call success. George Sheehan, an American physician, author, and running enthusiast, said, "Success means having the courage, the determination, and the will to become the person you believe you were meant to be." Earl Nightingale said, "Success is the progressive realization of a worthy goal or ideal." Obviously, success covers more than one area of your life—personal, professional, family, and even spiritual.

I believe it is well worth a little time to consider what success is and to be able to define what it is for you. Most people think of success as getting an education and then finding a good job that will pay them well. This is one of those definitions that came out of the Industrial Age and is becoming less applicable as our children and grandchildren grow up and begin careers.

I like what Bob Proctor, an internationally renowned motivational speaker, said about making money. He said you can make money at anything as long as you love what you're doing. You just have to know the strategies.

For an article in the Arizona Daily Star, teenagers were asked, "What do you think success is?" These teenagers defined success in several ways. They acknowledged that "many people define it as being financially wealthy with a big house and expensive cars." Others thought that personal success was more of a spiritual or service-centered life. They would follow their beliefs, and that would make them a success. Others think that seeing what needs to be done in society and then helping to change things for the better is what makes people successful.

People who think more about money as a measure of success believe that it will help them have what they consider a comfortable and happy lifestyle. In other words, they can do what they want and have what they want. Setting goals and then achieving them was also defined in the article as success.

FISHING FOR SUCCESS

I love the story about a Corsican fisherman. A businessman who was on vacation was walking down the beach. He came across the fisherman who sat on the beach with a fishing pole stuck in the sand.

"You could catch more fish if you used two poles," the businessman said to him.

"What would I do then?" the Corsican said.

The businessman thought this was easy to answer. "You could make extra money, buy a boat, and hire a crew," the businessman said. "Then you would catch even more fish and make even more money."

"What would I do after that?" said the fisherman.

"Well, you could own an entire fleet of fishing boats. Then you could sell to many restaurants and stores as a wholesaler. You would be rich and could do anything you want!" By this time the businessman was frustrated and was yelling at the fisherman.

The Corsican stretched and looked the other man in the face. "I'm doing what I want already!"

What a difference in their viewpoints of success! Most of these definitions and stories about success reveal that many of us associate successes with material or tangible things. For some, the more you have, the more successful you are. This is true in many ways. The purpose in learning strategies for money management is having practical ways of making your money work for you, as well as working for your money. Whatever you choose to do to earn money should be something you love doing. After you learn how to invest and have money working for you, you can work because you enjoy it, not because you have to work.

I've enjoyed all kinds of success, including financial success. I've experienced challenges at times, but I have learned from them and enjoy passing on what I've learned to others. I feel successful when I help others be successful. Now I'm reaping personal success by enjoying my son Bill, who is himself content with his work and accomplishments. I enjoy watching my daughter Sarah's success in writing her newest book. Sarah is also an entrepreneur in her own right and is becoming financially independent. Her great work with the Pearson Peacekeeping Center in Ottawa, Ontario, is admirable. My daughter Angela, who has contributed to the Landmark Education Corporation, is amazing. She is a computer whiz and uses her many talents in all that she does. My son Michael is finding his purpose in life, and I'm hopeful for his future. Last, but not least, I'm enjoying the personal success of my wife, Johanna, who has become a famous artist in the past nine years. I enjoy all of their successes. Each one of them brings me joy as I see them contributing to the betterment of humankind in so many ways, big and small.

I know people who believe that they are successful because they are wealthy in opportunities and possibilities. They have created wealth to share with other people who have less than they do. That makes them happy. They measure their successes by how happy they are, and whether they have helped other people become happy.

Choose to be happy.

"If, at the end of my life, I can attain only one type of success, I would not choose success in career, friends, money, status, or any other worldly goal. For what good are these to me without happiness? If, at the end of my life, I can look back and say, "I have contributed to the happiness of others and been happy myself," I will judge myself to have attained the most important kind of success."

—FROM *YOU CAN CHOOSE TO BE HAPPY*,
TOM G. STEVENS, PHD

I like Stevens's sentiment. For me personally, knowing that I have helped others achieve happiness is a great part of the success that I enjoy, along with my accomplishments and financial success.

This book mainly focuses on strategies for financial and professional success. You find happiness, satisfaction, and fulfillment when you enjoy success in all areas of your life. Maslow's hierarchy of needs teaches that when a person's basic needs are met, then he can move on to other things he wants. Good money management skills are the practical tools to meet all of your basic needs and to be able to get what you want beyond those basics.

MISTAKES ARE PART OF SUCCESS

Everyone makes mistakes. No one is going to do everything perfectly every time. This is an important point to remember. Here are some examples to illustrate this point.

Every one of the five hundred rich and successful people whom Napoleon Hill interviewed for his book, *Think and Grow Rich*, made some mistakes along the way. However, they still succeeded. They still had a successful attitude.

There are also many examples of how failure did not stop some of the most successful people in history. Thomas Edison spent $2 million inventing something that turned out to have very little value. Alexander Graham Bell's first attempts at the telephone didn't work. Many people attempted to invent the lightbulb before someone succeeded. The Wright brothers built several planes before they came up with the right design and combination of conditions to fly. The first submarines were very limited in their successes and ended up sinking to the bottom of the ocean.

One of the best-known American presidents was Abraham Lincoln. He was not successful in business. He was primarily self-taught and had only one year of formal schooling. He lost almost every election he ever ran for, including the state legislature, Congress, the Senate, and vice president. However, in 1860, Lincoln was elected president and governed during the years of the Civil War until his assassination. He's considered a great man.

Benjamin Disraeli is considered a great British statesman, but he was booed and hissed at until he returned to his seat during one of the first times he spoke in Parliament.

All of these mistakes or failures were bumps in the road on the way to success for these individuals. Their patience and their positive attitudes got them past the challenges.

Putting mistakes and failure into perspective means they aren't just negative things that happen to you. They are opportunities for learning so you'll know what *not* to do next time. These lessons may even point in the direction of *what you need to do*.

Improving your attitude is an inside job. Exercise a good and positive attitude often enough that you don't even have to think about it. In other words, a good attitude will eventually become your habitual way of being. If you have children, they will mirror your behaviour.

Sometimes success is inhibited by our negative attitudes toward other people and things. Sometimes those feelings are passed down from our parents, while others are formed by our own experiences. Judgments and prejudice seem to be passed down as well. They can be about individuals, other races or groups of people, places, or things. They aren't always based on real information or our own experiences.

For example, if your great-grandmother experienced someone being rude to her when she got off the boat from England, then your family has probably passed that story down from generation to generation. From that story you may think that people in that port city are rude to people who don't live there. You learn that people there are unfriendly.

As a result, you don't like them or their city. Your feelings aren't based on facts; they're based on one story of what your great-grandmother thought and felt. It has become a family attitude.

Family attitudes can be generational, and sometimes our attitudes about something stem from someone else's opinions formed by *their* experiences. I encourage you to be open to finding out more information about those attitudes. Find out whether a belief is valid or whether there is evidence that proves what you think is true. Remember, you are in charge of your own attitude!

THE LAW OF ATTRACTION

"To attract money, you must focus on wealth. It is impossible to bring more money into your life when you are noticing you do not have enough, because that means you are thinking *thoughts* that you do not have enough."

—RHONDA BYRNE

Have you ever noticed that even though you want different results, you tend to do the same thing and think the same way, yet expect the outcome to change? Are you surprised when you get the same old results? You need to change your way of thinking to change your results. This is called the Law of Attraction.

The Law of Attraction says energy is attracted to similar energies. When you think positive thoughts, you create an energy that attracts the same type of energy toward you. If you think negative thoughts, such as *I'm fat, I'm broke, I'm in debt,* then this is often what shows up in your life! You cause this energy to rush toward you!

Your thoughts become things. This is a powerful concept because it underlines the importance of having a positive self-image and a great attitude. The Law of Attraction works equally with positive or negative energy. If positive energy is being sent out, it will bring back positive energy. Conversely, negative energy attracts negative energy. One of the keys to applying the Law of Attraction in your life is to focus on what you want, rather than what you don't want.

HAVE–DO–BE

This concept of have–do–be is based on the belief that almost everyone has grown up believing that we must *have* some money to *do* the things that rich people do in order to *be* rich and live a quality lifestyle. In other words, we have to have something to do something to become something.

Motivational speaker Bob Proctor teaches a concept that I think is valuable. It is *be–do–have*. This concept is the opposite of what is typically taught. Bob's concept is different and much more powerful than the constrictive system of have–be–do.

BE–DO–HAVE

Using the be–do–have model, you see yourself *being* what you want (you cultivate the mind-set first), *doing* what you want in life (you do the things that you cultivated in your mind), and *having* what you want (your mind-set manifests in reality). Do you see the difference? If you believe you are rich and do the things that rich people do, such as manage your money, you will have riches. It's that simple.

So what do you want? Focus on what you want to have, what you want to do, and who you want to be.

Don't be fooled! This is a difficult task to learn because your mind always pictures what you don't want. So you must train yourself to think of what you do want. You will find that the visualization exercise is a good tool to help you with this task.

Rhonda Byrne is internationally known for her movie *The Secret* that highlights the Law of Attraction through the work of experts such as Bob Proctor, Lisa Nichols, and Marci Shimoff, among others. I encourage you to watch the movie, especially as a family, and discuss the Law of Attraction and how it has been working in your lives.

FAMILY SUCCESS CHECKLIST

$ Your self-image and attitude are linked together.

$ A positive attitude will take you further toward reaching your goals than a negative one.

$ *You* are completely in charge of your attitude.

$ You can keep the attitude you've always had or trade it in for a new and better one.

$ Work on yourself first.

$ The first step on your way to success is to develop a "can do" attitude.

$ You can learn from your mistakes and develop a success-focused attitude.

$ The Law of Attraction is at work all the time—put it to better use.

$ Your thoughts become things.

CHAPTER 4

SUCCESS FACTOR #1: TURNING OBSTACLES INTO OPPORTUNITIES

"When you allow yourself to begin to dream big dreams, creatively abandon the activities that are taking up too much of your time, and focus your inward energies on alleviating your main constraints, you start to feel an incredible sense of power and confidence."

—BRIAN TRACY

The next five chapters explain my five success factors. These factors, when practiced together, have allowed me to accomplish everything I have ever set my sights on. I'm going to explain each of the success factors and show you how to use them to accomplish your dreams.

What would your life be like a year from now if you consistently implemented my five success factors and achieved your dreams? What would your kids' lives be like watching you succeed in what you say you are going to do? Wow, hold onto that image.

OBSTACLES

We all know that in life we will be challenged at times. We will face circumstances that seem like obstacles that stand in our way of becoming what we want or getting what we want.

The following story describes a boy who did not see obstacles; he saw opportunities. A fourteen-year-old boy was too young to go to work in most places. He already knew what he wanted to do. He wanted to go to a university and study to be an architect. He had dreamed of designing and building homes and office buildings since he was eight years old. However, his family struggled with their finances, and his parents always told him that they didn't know how they could afford to send him to college. He was determined that he wouldn't let his parents' lack of money or encouragement get in his way.

This young man started mowing lawns for his neighbors. He paid his father for the gasoline and saved up for a lawn mower. First, he bought a used one. A friend's dad taught him to work on it and keep it in top condition. Soon the neighbors were so pleased with his work and his diligence that they recommended him to their friends. That meant he would need transportation to get to their homes. He didn't have a driver's license yet, and his dad didn't want to use the gas to take him to his jobs. He would walk a mile or more to some of his customers, pushing the lawn mower and carrying the gas can.

Toward the end of the summer, he realized that his source of income would run out when the weather got cold. He had made several hundred dollars over the summer and put it into a savings account. He spent very little on himself. Living in an area that usually got quite a bit of snow each winter, he decided to adapt his business to the market and the season. During the fall, he raked leaves and helped winterize gardens. By the first snowfall, the young man had invested in a snowblower. He told all of his regular customers about his winter services. Through his own efforts and perseverance, he built a small business with a good income.

By the second summer, he had more customers than he could handle by himself. He invested his money in two new lawn mowers and hired a friend to work with him to handle the customers he didn't have time for. The month after he got his driver's license, he purchased a used truck. He kept working and expanding his business until he finished high school and applied to the university. The fall after he graduated high school, he had saved enough money for the first two years of college. He had made a start for himself and invested in his business to make it grow. The best part is that he sold his year-round yard-care business to a competitor before he left for school and had enough to pay for his third and final year at the university. This young man is now a successful businessman who is accumulating wealth and living a successful life. He used the same strategies you are learning.

Too many times, people are willing to give up when they face obstacles. These people spend their lives making excuses for not making their dreams come true. Do you know one of these types? I want to put an end to that way of thinking—right here, right now.

What you see as an obstacle may be the biggest opportunity you've ever had on your road toward achieving your dreams. Obstacles are considered insurmountable depending only on the perspective that you take. Change your perspective, and the obstacle changes, too. In the same way that we think the people in our lives change after we have completed a personal-development course, so too do obstacles change only when we change. This is a good example of a shift in paradigm. Suddenly we see an opportunity rather than an obstacle.

When it comes to physical obstacles, there is often a way to the other side. If you come across a deep river, you can choose to go over it, around it, or even through it if you need to. The river can become a path on your adventure with the proper swimming or canoeing skills. It will stop you, however, if you choose to do nothing. When you stop and do not choose how to surmount the obstacle, you have lost. The river doesn't care if you choose or not—it is busy being a river and following its natural laws.

The same holds true with other obstacles. Remember how I was asked to leave high school? I truly was uneducated at age fourteen, with no future prospects in sight. I thought my uneducated status was an obstacle to my success. My brother Gerry stayed in school and excelled. My parents were proud of him. He was proud of himself. He was smart. His education wasn't an obstacle; it was his opportunity. With Gerry as my character foil in my early years, I couldn't help but think that my uneducated status was an obstacle.

I refused to accept that this obstacle was going to stop me. I decided to choose other educational options that worked for me. I went to trade school and learned how to be a carpenter. I apprenticed with a master carpenter and added to my level of education. I hung out with people who were equally educated, so we were all moving in the same life direction. Fewer book-smart people were around me to call me dumb. I took real estate courses and learned skills for making money in that industry. I refreshed my knowledge at least once a year through professional development courses. I practiced my craft—even though my craft has changed over the years. I left behind my doubts about my capacity to be educated and the negative feelings I had about school. I replaced them every time I overcame an obstacle that might have hindered my goal of becoming successful. As my perspective changed, so did my obstacles.

Obstacles are different for all people. However, one of the most common obstacles to becoming rich is many adults' belief that they can't understand money management. In fact, the belief is so strong that they make it into an obstacle for their children. Because schools don't teach the secrets we're discussing, it's up to you to pass them on. Why depend on school for something so important? Guarantee your child's financial prosperity yourself. Some people don't know any better than what they were taught by parents who barely made it from paycheck to paycheck, or have learned through the school of hard knocks. I promise that trial-and-error methods will put more obstacles in your path toward riches than using the money management skills presented in the next chapter.

A generational lack of knowledge that passes from parent to child is one obstacle that kept people in the twentieth century from becoming wealthy. Basically, the adults didn't know any better and passed on what little they knew to their children. In some cases, they didn't really pass on anything except how to survive in a world that offers one challenge after another. Fortunately, we have the antidote for that in teaching our kids financial skills that will make a difference in their futures.

The biggest obstacle to your success is your mind-set if it holds you back from being successful. We live in a time that is full of opportunities, but we must choose to take them. I really like the way Robert Kiyosaki shows the difference between his rich dad and his poor dad. For those of you who haven't read *Rich Dad, Poor Dad*, Kiyosaki's biological father, whom he refers to as his "poor dad," had multiple educational degrees and worked hard his whole life. Kiyosaki's "rich dad" is actually his best friend's father, who worked smart and had a completely different mindset and way of looking at money. Both dads had good intentions, but at age nine, Kiyosaki decided to listen and learn from his rich dad about money management and business. The outcome was that he created wealth, success, and happiness for himself and his family, rather than for an institution, organization, or corporation.

Turn obstacles into opportunities. Help your children to see obstacles as opportunities.

FAMILY SUCCESS CHECKLIST

$ What you see as an obstacle may be the biggest opportunity you've ever had.

$ Your thinking can turn an obstacle into an opportunity that you can handle.

$ Facing challenges and making mistakes can lead to your success.

CHAPTER 5

SUCCESS FACTOR #2: MAKING GOOD DECISIONS

Making good decisions in life can help you achieve success faster. I know it has helped me to accomplish my goals.

Wouldn't it be great for our children and teenagers to know how to make good decisions for themselves in all aspects of their lives? Wouldn't it be good to teach our children how to make smart decisions using their money management skills? One of the obstacles that young people (and some adults) face is that they don't know how to make good decisions for themselves.

To start with, they confuse making choices with making decisions. We make choices in seconds. For example, you may choose to have chicken rather than leftover soup for dinner tonight. There isn't much to consider; you choose based on your feelings at the moment. However, a decision takes consideration. You look at some kind of information and weigh it before you make a decision.

Learning to make good decisions can be a trial-and-error process if you don't have anyone to teach you the process. Decisions themselves can teach you a lesson if you let them. If you make a mistake, you can learn from it and know not to do that again. However, if you don't learn as part of the mistake process, then you are destined to make the same mistakes over and over again. Hence, learning is a part of making good decisions.

This next section offers some tips on how to make better decisions. The goal is to reduce the percentage of poorly made decisions and replace them with good decisions. Major decisions such as where your kids want to attend university, where you want to live, finding a career path, short-listing investment options, whom to marry, and having children are all important and life-changing decisions that can cause you to fail or make you successful. Which would you rather be?

INFLUENCING FACTORS

You may think that when you make a decision that you are doing it yourself. The truth is that everyone is influenced by external elements, and these influence the decisions that we make.

Values

Values are your established ideals of life. You and your family have a set of values. Society has a set of values. You and your friends have a set of values.

Peers

Your peers share the same age, ability, and grade or work that you do, as well as interests and cultural identity.

Habits

Habits are your patterned ways in which you think and do things. Habits can be constructive (eating healthy meals) or destructive (smoking), positive and negative.

Feelings

Feelings are your emotional guidance system. They are your brain's way of telling you what feels good for you and what feels bad for you. These can include love, anger, frustration, hope, depression, etc.

Ego

Your ego serves self-gratification and is a strong influence in making decisions.

Family

Your family can be made up of many types of people and is usually defined as parents and their children. You may have an adopted family, a blood-relation family, and a virtual family.

Risks and Consequences

A risk is a chance of loss, and consequences are the results of a potential risk. Ask yourself, "What or how much can I stand to win?" and "What or how much can I stand to lose?" when making a decision.

There are risks with any decision. Risk taking can be a very healthy activity, and you should be aware of the types of risk common to financial decision making. These include personal risk, inflation risk, interest rate risk, income risk, liquidity risk, and changes in government policy and laws.

Age

Your age can influence your decision-making process. Many choices in life are age-dependent (opening your own bank account, driving, voting, marriage). Age can even influence how much you know about something, although not always.

MAKING YOUR MOVE

To make a good decision, use the following list of statements to move you from the educational stage toward the decision:

1. The decision I want to make presents me with a series of options. These options are:

2. My research regarding each of the options suggests that:

3. I prefer the following option:

4. I prefer it because:

5. I have made a similar decision before and have learned that:

6. My wife, partner, kids, parents, etc. would prefer I make the following decision:

7. My preferred decision will effect the following people:

8. If my preferred decision causes effects, they are known to be:

9. To my knowledge, the negative effects of making this decision are:

10. I will make the following decision by the following date:

Use the list for something that you want to make a decision about now. Use a simple example from your life, such as deciding which summer camp to send your kids to this year or whether to go home for Christmas (well, maybe that one isn't so simple).

When making a decision, consider whether it violates others' rights. Are you making your decision in competition with another person or because that's what is best for you? Some decisions may take more time than others. Learn to understand what influences your decision making; it will help you be successful in all aspects of your life. Imagine knowing this from a young age and being able to apply it to business decisions and investments. Believe me; this will make a difference for you and your children.

Be careful not to use your old mind-set when making new decisions. Sometimes that little voice can influence you by saying, "You can't do this yet because you can't afford it." I've learned that after you decide to go ahead with your plans, you can always find or attract what you need financially.

FAMILY SUCCESS CHECKLIST

$ Take the time to consider all the information for a good decision.

$ Successful people can and do make decisions—every day.

$ Everyone—adults, teens, and kids—need to follow the steps of good decision making.

$ Use the decision-making statements to see the learning opportunities that are inherent in the process of making good decisions.

CHAPTER 6

SUCCESS FACTOR #3: SETTING GOALS

"If one advances confidently in the direction of his dreams,and endeavors to live the life which he has imagined,he will meet with a success unexpected in common hours."

—HENRY DAVID THOREAU

Setting goals is my favourite success factor. Heck, if I hadn't set goals as a kid, I wouldn't be where I am today. People who don't set regular goals are like boats without rudders. The water and wind take them wherever they are moving. Do you know people who are rudderless? It's simple to set goals. True happiness requires some planning. Plan for happiness. This chapter shows you how.

Begin by thinking about what you want. What is your dream? Do you want to be a successful entrepreneur making $1 million per year after taxes? Do you want to be a humanitarian who relieves suffering in places such as Haiti and Afghanistan? What about being the best mom who takes pride in educating her children to become financially free?

Your next task is to write down a few of your biggest, most beautiful dreams. Then, when you feel that one of them is just right, use it when we turn our attention to setting goals. Having a dream that will be realized through the completion of goals is the best place to begin.

GOALS

Goals are things for which an effort is made and, when achieved, are cause for celebration. Goals are things that you want to achieve in order to realize your dream. In other words, your dream is the overarching idea, such as "I want to be a millionaire," while the goals are the actions you take to fulfill your dream.

In many sports, goals are the activities that give a team points to determine a winner. Goals are also referred to as "crossing the finish line," "score," "home run," and "touchdown." The more goals a team achieves, the more they win their games—or in your case, achieve your dreams.

Goals are best understood in relation to timelines. You can set goals that are short, medium, and long term in nature. The most successful people in the world know what their five-year goals are. Some even know what their lifetime goals are. Using the following timelines, think about what goals you have that contribute to your big dream.

- Short-term goals (one to four weeks)

- Medium-term goals (two to twelve months)

- Long-range goals (one year or longer)

Goals are described in short statements. Goal statements describe the activities you will do to get the thing you want. Goal setting creates the framework you will use to reach your goals. The goal of a soccer game is to score goals, but if there were no goalposts, no one would know how to score. When you set goals, you create your own goalposts.

The most successful goal statements have the following elements:

Present tense

Emotional

Realistic

Measurable

Action-based

And that spells PERMA—which is short for permanent. If your goal statement has these elements, the more easily you will get the thing that you want.

Here are some PERMA goals:

"I am so excited now that I have bought my first used car with my own $5,000."

"I am grateful that I spent my anniversary with my spouse in Hawaii."

"I am thrilled that I live in my dream home that is completely paid for."

To help you write you own PERMA goals, here are a few helpful hints:

P: PRESENT TENSE

In the old days, goal statements were written in the future tense: "By December 31, I *will* be able to run 10 kilometers," or " On or before July 30, I *will* have money in my riches account." But our brains don't think the future tense is very believable. So now we put goal statements into the present tense so our brains believe our goals and want to help us achieve them.

"I am ..." *not* "I will be ..."

"I know ..." *not* "I will know ..."

"I have ..." *not* "I will have ..."

"Now that I ..." *not* "When I ..."

E: EMOTIONAL

Why include feelings? Our brains don't want to do anything unless it feels good. So we have to build emotions into our goal statements.

"I am so happy and grateful …"

"I am excited that …"

"I feel terrific because …"

R: REALISTIC

Financial goals should be realistic. For example, if you want to be a millionaire, it won't realistically happen by next month. However, you may want to have money in your savings account in six months. This is a realistic goal for a young person or an adult starting on the road to financial freedom.

M: MEASURABLE

Be sure to add measurable amounts of money to your goal statement. This defines your goal and puts it into a context that makes sense.

"I have $1,000 …"

"I now have $10,000 in my savings account …"

"I can buy a great used car with my $5,000 savings …"

A: ACTION-BASED

If you can build an activity into your goal statement, it is more believable. It also gives you the instructions your brain requires so you don't forget what you need to do to achieve your goal.

"I actively ..."

"Every day I pay ..."

"I save ..."

When you are goal setting, your goal must be bigger than you are. Those goals have an emotional attachment to achieve. For example, you want to save enough money to take your whole family on a dream vacation. It is for more than just you, so by including your family, you add those powerful feelings.

ACHIEVING GOALS IS CAUSE FOR CELEBRATION

In my own experience of building up a construction business, a real estate business, and a ski resort, among others, I know that it takes time, effort, and focus to get from writing a goal down to achieving it.

Basic goal setting is a skill that you can use at any age. This skill will help you end up where you really want to be. The best place to can start is by knowing what is important to you. Sit down with your notebook and brainstorm what you want to do for the rest of your life. I recommend that you do this as a family. Each person will have different ideas that are unique to them. Parents need to do this also. You will find goal-setting sheets in the Activities section at the end of the book that you can complete with your children.

For big goals, it's a good idea to set up mini-goals that are steps to the overall goal. It gives you a road map to follow and checkpoints along the way that let you know how you're doing. It also helps you to stay focused and to persevere. You can celebrate all the small successes along the way.

With the busy schedules that families have, if your goal is one more thing to do every day, it may be the straw that breaks the camel's back. My point is that overcommitment can get overwhelming. As a parent, you not only manage your own schedule, but also those of your children. A friend of mine kept a master calendar for her family with each person's schedule posted in a different color to keep everyone straight. When you are setting goals, they need to fit into your daily schedule. That's why it is so important to be fully committed to your goals. Set priorities and get rid of the things on your schedule that are time consuming and distracting. Setting goals and achieving them should be fun—just like scoring a touchdown!

Setting goals and achieving them are based on your self-image and your attitude, which you read about in earlier chapters. When you think better of yourself and have more self-confidence, you can improve your track record and know that you can achieve the goals you set. This factor is important to you as a successful goal achiever.

You can develop your own process after you and your kids have learned how to go through it from start to finish. You will be surprised at how much your kids will learn about themselves, as well as what they really want and are willing to commit to achieving through these activities. Families that follow this guide to success achieve riches sooner.

When you take the first step down the road that ends at your goal, the Law of Attraction will pick up on the energy and start working for you. The other steps you need to complete your goal will come to you along the way.

Because each age group has different goals that are appropriate for it, you will be achieving and creating new goals all the time. I do caution you to focus on one major goal at a time so you can dedicate yourself to achieving your goal, not just coming close.

ACHIEVING YOUR GOAL

It's challenging to set big goals and see them all the way through. You will encounter challenges and possible delays along the way, but those can't stop you. You may need to adjust your direction as you move toward the goal. It's like flying from Toronto to Florida. The pilot has to make a few course corrections along the way so you arrive in Miami, Florida, instead of Atlanta, Georgia. The path to successfully achieving your goal will involve adjustments. Things you learn along the way may give you a more efficient way of reaching the result. They might save you money and time. It would be a bad practice to just keep doing what you're doing to get to the end if you have found a better way during the process.

Unfortunately, sometimes people get tired of pushing toward the goal. They can still see it, but the goal isn't as clear as it was in the beginning. When you set your goal, you must have complete clarity about what the end result is to be or look like. Some people get close enough to almost see what they want, but then give up and settle for where they are. One reason people stop in sight of the goal is that deep inside they believe that they can't have what they really want. This is like running a race and coming up to the finish line, but not crossing it! That's not the smartest way to run a race.

There is a story about a young man in India who wanted to learn from a holy man. One day the holy man took the young man out into the river. Then the holy man held his head under the water. At first the young man thought about what kind of lesson he was supposed to be learning from the experience. After a while, he grew concerned that the holy man wasn't loosening his grip or letting him up out of the water. As the young man's body began to strain for air, he finally began thrashing and fighting against the holy man. He overturned the holy man and made it to the surface, gasping for air. As the two stumbled out of the water to the shore, the young man looked at the holy man not understanding. The holy man stopped, looked into his eyes, and said, "When you want enlightenment as much as you wanted air, then you are ready to learn."

The lesson from this story is that when you have a goal, you need to be completely committed to it emotionally. Your commitment has to go beyond thinking it's a good idea or intellectually weighing the pros and cons of deciding to do this thing or not. You have to want to achieve the goal as much as you want and need your next breath of air.

Some of the kids who come into our seminars don't seem to be as excited as their parents at first, but the activities draw them in, and they learn tremendous lessons while they are having fun. Many parents tell us afterward that they can see the change in their children almost immediately. They learn how to set goals, plan, and look ahead to a successful and rich future.

When you achieve a goal, you feel great doing it. Don't think the only important part of achievement is the end result. Yes, the result is important. However, I encourage people to learn lessons *along* the way and enjoy the process. We are here for the enjoyment of the journey. You'll find life much more satisfying if that's the way you live. Your children will watch you and learn the same lesson.

FAMILY SUCCESS CHECKLIST

$ Setting goals gives you direction.

$ Achieving goals gives you success.

$ Setting and achieving goals begins with an idea.

$ The idea is followed up with action and perseverance.

$ Choose goals that you are emotionally attached to and passionate about.

$ Be totally committed to achieving your goal.

$ Set mini-goals to achieve your overall goal.

$ Celebrate your successes!

CHAPTER 7

SUCCESS FACTOR #4: PERSEVERANCE

Like Bob Proctor, I know that perseverance makes goals happen. Without perseverance, people stop before crossing the finish line. I learned perseverance on the farm. If I didn't get into that pigsty and muck it out, I'd get into big trouble with my dad. However, even though I was deathly afraid of the pigs—heck they were big, ugly, stinky, and did I mention big?—I persevered until the sty was clean. If I didn't persevere, I would just be delaying the inevitable. Dad would make me do it or else! The perseverance I learned on the farm has been with me all my life. Although I am no longer motivated to persevere because of fear, I persevere so that I meet my goals and achieve success that much sooner. Don't delay the inevitable!

One of the qualities to instill in your children is that of perseverance. Perseverance is the ability to see things through, from start to finish.

I'd like to share a story about perseverance that I learned when I was twenty-one years old.

I was invited to join the local Kiwanis Club. This worldwide organization helps to raise money for particular functions and charities in their communities. Our club had about twenty members. At the beginning of my second year, I was elected to be the Ways and Means chairman. My mandate was to come up with a project to raise money for a charity that the club would support for that year.

The Kiwanis Club was fairly new to our area. There was also a Lions Club in the town that was well entrenched with at least sixty members. That meant we were both in competition to raise money in our small town. I'd never done this kind of charitable work before, so it was a new experience.

To fulfill my role as Ways and Means chairman, I had an idea to offer mixed nuts for sale that would be delivered the week before Christmas. I proposed the idea to the other members at one of our weekly meetings.

I couldn't believe the naysayers who shot my idea down with their negative comments! They were convinced that there was no way this would work. According to them, the Lions Club sold chocolate-covered nuts for Christmas and had the whole town pretty well tied up.

The next day, I decided to go to the nut company in Toronto myself and talk to someone there. The person I spoke with at the company suggested that we also offer licorice allsorts so people had a choice. I thought that was a great idea—in fact, it may even increase sales.

I made another presentation to the Kiwanis, telling them what I had found out. They almost booed me out of the room! They said, "Who buys licorice allsorts for Christmas? The Lions Club will make us look like fools." Of course, these responses set off all kinds of chatter in my head. I thought, "Do I need this?" Here I was doing volunteer work, and I got that kind of abuse. I was ready to give the Kiwanis Club a piece of my mind, but I bit my tongue. I decided instead to talk to some of my neighbors and see if I could sell mixed nuts and licorice allsorts.

One autumn evening after dinner, I started out on my task of offering mixed nuts and licorice allsorts to raise money for the Kiwanis Club. I drove around the block three times because I was afraid to get out of my car and knock on the first door. Finally, I stopped my car and sat there wondering if I would go knock on the door or not. Then I remembered something I had learned at a seminar—if you are afraid to make cold calls in your given neighborhood, roll down your car window and throw your car keys out the window onto the front lawn of the house. When you go pick up your keys, keep on walking right up to the house and knock on the first door!

I did exactly that for the first door. Then I did it again for the second door and the third door. Each time the answer was the same. They said, "No, we buy from the Lions Club." I felt totally devastated and rejected.

I went back to my car, ripped open the packages of nuts and the licorice allsorts and started eating them myself. They were really tasty! Then an idea hit me that changed my whole approach. I opened a package of each and decided to show the potential customer the products and give them a taste, too.

When I went to the next house, I said to the resident, "You probably buy chocolate-covered nuts from the Lions Club. However, we Kiwanians are offering mixed nuts and licorice allsorts, and you won't have to pay for them until we deliver them to you about a week before Christmas. Try a sample. Which would you like, the licorice or a box of nuts?" In about an hour and a half, I had sold more than one hundred fifty boxes.

My next presentation at our weekly meeting was a whole lot different. The Kiwanis Club accepted my idea. That Christmas our club made more than $2,500 profit from the sales.

The experience taught me to persevere despite obstacles. Think about it—not only did I not have the support of my club, I didn't have the support of the first few potential customers. Worst of all, I nearly didn't have my own support! I persevered in spite of these obstacles, however, and accomplished my goal as Ways and Means chairman. I thank God that I had the courage to throw my keys on the first front lawn and start knocking on doors!

WHAT WILL BE YOUR MOTIVATION?

It is critical for you to understand the motivation that causes you to persevere. You need to be crystal clear on this point. What will cause you to wake up at 4:30 AM to organize your presentation to your biggest client? What will cause you to be patient and understanding with your children as you teach them about money management? What will motivate you to make call after call after call until you find the money you need for your big deal?

What stops one person from achieving her goal to become wealthy while another person reaches that goal? Perseverance through the good times and the bad times. It is the most valuable skill to cultivate in yourself and your kids. See things through, from beginning to end. Cross the finish line.

FAMILY SUCCESS CHECKLIST

$ Perseverance is a proven skill of the rich.

$ Perseverance means seeing something through from beginning to end.

$ Discover what will motivate you to persevere, no matter what.

$ Perseverance will get you across the finish line.

$ Teach your kids to persevere until they achieve success.

The Main Street village shoppes built by Doug Meharg in the early 1980s.

The former Century 21 office and plaza, built by Doug in the early '90s.

CHAPTER 8

SUCCESS FACTOR #5: VISUALIZATION

I have found visualization to be a great tool to increase my self-image and confidence over the years. Let me teach you how to put visualization to work in your life.

Visualization is a process of closing your eyes and imagining a scene or circumstance that has you as the main actor undertaking a series of actions. For example, athletes use visualization to imagine their successful completion of a competition. Skiers use it to see themselves cresting every hill, carving past every racing pole, and zooming past the finish line with their specific time flashing on the digital display. Divers use it to imagine every twist and flip, as well as the minimal splash they make as they enter the water. Numerous scientific experiments have linked visualization with the positive outcome of the event being visualized. In simple terms, if you can see your goal before it happens, rehearsing it in your mind, the likelihood of accomplishing it multiplies!

Visualization is linked with your self-image. When you rehearse something in your mind's eye, it becomes easier and less frightening. This increases your self-image and confidence because you have already successfully completed the action in your mind.

Visualization can be used in areas of our lives other than sports. I use it to improve my health, my wealth, and my happiness. I was a runner when I first learned about visualization. I weighed 198 pounds. I used the technique to see myself in better shape and weighing a healthier weight. In twenty-one days, I was down to 180 pounds without a diet or changing my habits. It intrigued me that visualization could work so well for me. The dreams and goals that I don't visualize don't happen.

My daughter Sarah and her husband have successfully used visualization to picture their perfect oceanfront property and dream job on the East Coast. They employed visualization to find the perfect home and job to maximize their experience living on the ocean. Their visualization included a two-story barn and a large six-bedroom house with a view of gorgeous sunsets over the ocean. They envisioned a large and bright modern kitchen with high countertops, lots of built in cupboards, and a gas range stove. For fun, they visualized two hot tubs (one indoors and one on the back deck). They also visualized having good relationships with great neighbors. A short time later, Sarah got her dream job as the senior researcher for the Pearson Peacekeeping Center, and she and her husband moved into the very home with all the features in their visions. These jobs and properties are rare finds on the East Coast, yet my daughter and her spouse manifested their visions into reality.

Before we go any further, let me tell you a powerful story of how I used visualization to close a $43 750 000 deal.

I DIDN'T KNOW MUCH ABOUT GOLF

I have belonged to an investment club for approximately forty-five years. About fifteen years ago, one of the members asked my advice on the possible sale of his golf course. I was pleased to give him some advice, even though my real estate company specialized in residential sales. I wasn't involved in such large real estate transactions like a big golf course.

Over the next week, I thought about the advice I had given my friend. I thought, "I should do a big real estate deal like that." Nothing was stopping me; I just hadn't done such a deal before. Right then and there I decided that I was going to sell that beautiful fifty-four–hole golf course for the owner.

I acquired all the necessary information on this golf course so I could talk intelligently to any prospects who might be interested in such a purchase. Now, I didn't have a clue to whom I would offer this golf course. At that time I was not a golfer; therefore, I didn't know whether it was a championship golf course, and further, I did not have a written listing from the owner offering it for sale. And for those of you unfamiliar with real estate deals, that's a bad thing.

I was at a loss. What should I do to sell this course? Suddenly, it dawned on me that I could use visualization to assist me in making a deal.

I set about it systematically. Over the next two years, I put my skills to work. I found a nice, quiet place to conduct my visualization. I would calm myself by breathing deeply with my eyes closed. I would then imagine a group of people in my office transacting the golf course deal. I had developed a clear image of these people, not even knowing who they were. I could imagine what they were wearing and how they interacted with me and each other. I could even see their happy, successful faces as they agreed to the exact price my friend wanted for his golf course.

At that time, I was also involved in building a forty-eight-unit condo, which was located near a lake. I decided to buy a powerboat that could be used to take prospective condo buyers on short tours. Installed on this boat was a type of computer for water navigation, which was called a "Loran C." I didn't know how to work such a complex piece of new technology, so I called one of my associate friends who was a real estate broker in the Century 21 system from Oakville, Ontario. He was a boater and knew all about this type of navigational equipment. I asked him if he would teach me how to operate the equipment. He invited me to the west end of Toronto where we would have lunch and I would get instructions on the equipment.

Just before hanging up the phone, to my astonishment he said, "By the way, do you know if there are any golf courses in your area that are for sale?"

"As a matter of fact, I certainly do!" I said.

Can you believe that out of the blue someone I knew had buyers who wanted the exact golf course that my friend wanted to sell?

Perhaps it wasn't out of the blue at all. At that time I had forgotten about the Law of Attraction. However, visualization reminded me that the Law of Attraction was at work—even when I didn't think about the golf course. Though I may not have realized it at the time, what I know now is that the Law of Attraction truly works.

During a back-and-forth negotiation period between the buyer and the seller, I had both parties meet in my office *exactly* the way I pictured it in my mind from my visualization sessions over a two-year period. The deal was finalized within four hours, and a sale took place for the price of $43 750 000. Did I mention that this was the exact price that the owner wanted?

That was the largest sale that I ever completed. I believe because of my visualization and continued focus that I was *set up* to make it happen. Visualization works for me, and it *will* work for you.

VISUALIZATION 101

To begin this process, get a notebook and answer these questions:

When I am successful, I will be wearing ...

When I am successful, I will be doing ...

When I am successful, I will have ...

I'm not talking about a to-do list, but a dream list. Go full hog! What is your heart of hearts seeing for you? For your family? For your futures?

Now think of something that you would like to accomplish based on this exercise. Maybe it is the perfect deal or perhaps making a speech or buying your dream car.

Next, sit in a chair with your hands resting on your thighs. Close your eyes. Keep your eyes focused on a fictitious point in your mind. Breathe deeply for ten breaths.

Think in pictures of the situation you have decided to use for this visualization exercise. For learning purposes, I offer an example of buying a car. While you review the example, keep in mind that is the visualization has a beginning, a middle, and an end.

VISUALIZING YOUR DREAM CAR

See yourself at the dealership selecting your car with the interior you want and the paint color you've always dreamed of. The car is loaded with everything, including GPS and movie screens for the children's entertainment on trips. It has heated seats for those cold winter nights (heck, I'm Canadian. I think about these things!). Now picture yourself smiling and relaxed. You've got a very fat savings account that was intended just for this purpose. Imagine yourself choosing the car. Then see yourself writing a check for the car. The salesman hands you the keys, smiles, and congratulates you on your fabulous taste in luxury vehicles. You drive away from the dealership in your dream car and drive along the perfect cruising road. It is beside the ocean, and it curves and banks in all the right places. You can see your hands gripping the leather steering wheel. The car smells of beautiful newness. You feel giddy and gleeful! What a rush! The car is yours to keep. You earned it, and you deserve every bit of it.

LOSING EIGHTEEN POUNDS IN TWENTY-ONE DAYS

I used to be a runner. About thirty years ago, I weighed 198 pounds. I guess I wasn't really overweight, but felt I was too heavy for running.

I used to run three or four days a week. At the time, I was taking one of Bob Proctor's seminars. One evening the topic was on visualization. I went home and puzzled over what I could try my new skill on. I needed something that was measurable—that way I would believe that visualization worked like Bob said it would. I decided to try it on my weight.

I felt that my ideal weight for running was 180 pounds. So I took the instructions and visualized being slim and weighing 180 pounds. I imagined myself feeling slim, looking slim, and running slim. For twenty-one consecutive days—morning and evening—I got into a relaxed state of mind and did my visualization.

I did not change my eating habits except for a thing or two, like switching from cream to milk in my coffee. After a few days of consistent, intense visualization, I miraculously lost the desire to eat some foods like ice cream and sweets (my favourites!).

In twenty-one days, I weighed myself. I was 180 pounds! Apparently, because of my visualization, I activated my metabolism. Since then I've maintained 180 pounds with little effort. That's thirty years of powerful weight loss, handled in twenty-one days!

I was consistent, diligent, and followed Bob's instructions to the letter. It worked for me, and I know it will work for you.

VISUALIZATION SUMMARY

This is the kind of exercise that gets you completely involved. With practice and repetition, you will be able to see the car, feel the leather seats, smell the new car smell, hear the great sound system, and feel the wind blowing through your hair as you zoom down the highway with the top down. You will get excited and energized just thinking about your goal after you have ended the visualization. Science tells us that our bodies don't know the difference between the real and the visualized experience. It feels the same. When you feel it, you believe it, and you will begin living for it and seeing the results of your visualizations.

This is powerful knowledge. Visualization is so powerful in creating the riches you want and deserve because it takes your ideas and thoughts and gives them substance. Your thoughts energize your emotions, which causes you to act, which creates your results.

VISUALIZING FOR ADULTS AND KIDS

Learning to visualize as an adult can be more difficult than for a child. Children and young people have great imaginations and creativity. Their minds are full of dreams and visions of who they want to be and what they want to do. Work to develop that as a life skill in your children. If you are reading this as a young person, then keep using your power of visualization. Don't give it up because someone tells you it's time to grow up and leave your imaginary future behind. If you can visualize it, then with the right focus and actions you can make dreams become reality. You can choose your future.

FAMILY SUCCESS CHECKLIST

$ Visualization is linked with your self-image.

$ Choose one goal to visualize twice a day for thirty days. See yourself successful and doing all the things that successful people do.

$ Visualization can help you focus on what you want, not on what you don't want. This will improve your life.

$ Teach your kids to visualize.

$ If you can visualize it, you can choose your future.

House built by Doug Meharg in 1967, which he still lives in today.

The public school Doug attended, now a restaurant called "The School."

CHAPTER 9

MONEY MANAGEMENT

"Like water, food, air and housing, [money] affects everything, yet, for some reason, the world of academics thinks it's a subject below their social standing."

—ROBERT KIYOSAKI

Now that you know my five success factors, the next step is to teach you about money management. As I mentioned in the Introduction, money management is not my unique idea. It has been practiced for centuries, and it is a known wealth-creation tool. Few use the system; yet when they do, they can be, do, and have almost anything they want in life.

I've found that children, even young ones, can learn the basics of money and how to manage it. They can learn the principle of saving from a very young age. Little children may not understand the system presented in this chapter, but you will. You can help your youngest kids by starting with a personal piggy bank and the concept of saving—which we will go over in this chapter. Older children and teens can easily learn from my money management system. If you're reading this, then you've got the tools in your hands to help your children learn the key to becoming rich.

As a parent I passed on these lessons to my own children, although my daughters may disagree. My fault was that I taught the lesson only once or twice. Real learning comes from practice and repetition. Sure, my girls were savers—they learned that from me—but I didn't give them a system through which to do the saving! Well, oversights aside, I've now perfected the system and have put it in black and white so it is clear to you and your kids.

Parents whom I've talked with sometimes have concerns over sharing too much financial information with their kids. Some are afraid their kids will see how unorganized they are with the family's finances, while others feel as if this is private information. They feel that all the details of their income, investments, and expenses don't need to be spread out in front of their children. I respect and understand their feelings. I'm not asking you to reveal things that may not be age appropriate. What I am asking is that you read this chapter and then work through the activities with your children so they know the principles and can use the skills of money management to their best advantage.

One parent shared with me that she played Monopoly with her children when they were growing up to help them understand money management. You may have read about this strategy in other books or magazine articles. During a game one Friday evening, one of the children asked about buying a toy he really wanted. When the mother said they couldn't afford it this week, the boy pursued the request by asking, "Don't you still have checks in your checkbook?" That was when she decided to show the children how the money was spent each month.

She gave each child $1,000 in Monopoly money. Then she asked them what they needed to pay first. Of course, her son mentioned the toy. She discussed what had to be paid for them to enjoy life every day. Then she went over the basics of the bills and necessities. If anything was left over, she had a list of things they had wanted to do and have. The children were astounded when they ran out of Monopoly money before they could pay for everything they thought they wanted. Then she introduced the idea of putting some of the money into savings every payday. They still could pay their bills but would save the money they needed for things like the toy her son wanted. At the time, this single mother didn't know the concepts I'm teaching here, but she has since learned them and is teaching her grandchildren how to pay themselves first and save.

I mean, really—are you going to be happy when your young adult calls home from college in a panic asking for rent money because he blew his funds on refreshments? How many kids graduate and go away to university and are constantly calling home for more money? How many of them are on their own for the first time? Wouldn't you like to know that your children are prepared to go out into the world? Spending is fun when we know the right skills for saving. And for a young adult, starting out on his own can be empowering, especially if he knows how to live life on his own terms. The system in this chapter will prepare you to help your children to do so.

MONEY WORKING FOR MONEY?

When I was seventeen years old, I read a book called *The Richest Man in Babylon*. The basic idea of the book is to teach people to pay themselves first, at least 10 percent of all the money they receive during their lifetime. In addition to saving, it said the money should be put to work so it earns more money for you. Most of us work five days a week, forty hours a week. Some of us work more hours than that, but no one can work twenty-four hours every day of the week. When you put your money to work for you through good investments, your money works for you twenty-four hours a day, seven days a week; that multiplies your sources of income. That works out to two days a week, or about 104 days a year, that your money is working for you while you are at home and enjoying time with your family and friends.

You don't have to be born into a family with old money to become wealthy on your own. You just need to follow the practice of paying yourself at least 10 percent as the first step in managing your money. I found that I could have everything I really needed and wanted with 90 percent of the money I earned.

THE TIME VALUE OF MONEY

Early on in this process, I learned about the time value of money. The time value of money is the relationship between the value of money over a period of time. Another way to look at the time value of money is by knowing that the earlier you start saving money, the more it will grow over time. Examine this table to understand this very important concept.

Name	Yearly savings	Age started saving	Age stopped saving	Years saved	Total investment	Interest rate	Savings at age 65
Connor	$2,000	22	31	9 years	$18,000	9%	$579,471
Jasmine	$2,000	31	65	35 years	$70,000	9%	$470,249

Jasmine's savings will never catch up to Connor's! Connor saved for only nine years, but because he started saving earlier, the compound interest allowed his money to grow faster than Jasmine's. This is why Albert Einstein said compound interest was the most powerful force in the world; he even referred to it as the Eighth Wonder of the World.

This is the time value of money at work. If your kids start saving money this month, and save only $2,000 a year for the next ten years, and then they stop putting money away but never touch that $20,000, they will retire rich and be millionaires.

THE EIGHTH WONDER OF THE WORLD

Money can earn interest in two ways: simple and compound interest. Simple interest is the amount earned on the original principal amount only. This type of interest rate is very seldom used. Compound interest is the interest paid on the original principal amount plus any interest earned. This means that you earn interest on your interest over and over again.

To calculate simple interest:

Principal x % interest rate x # of years = amount earned

If you had $100 in your savings account that paid 6 percent simple interest, during the first year you would earn $6:

$$\$100 \times 0.06 \times 1 = \$6$$

At the end of two years, you would have earned $12 of interest on your original $100, for a grand total of $112.

The account would continue to grow at a rate of 6 percent per year, despite the accumulated interest. In other words, you only make interest on the original $100 principal amount in a simple interest situation.

To calculate compound interest:

(Principal + earned interest) x % interest rate x # of years = amount earned

If you had $100 in your savings account that paid 6 percent interest compounded annually, during the first year you would earn $6 in interest:

$$\$100 \text{ x } 0.06 \text{ x } 1 = \$6$$

With compound interest, the second year you would earn $6.36 in interest. The calculation the second year is:

$$(\$100 + \$6) \text{ x } 0.06 \text{ x } 1 = \$6.36$$

Now the amount in your savings account is $112.36:

$$\$106 + \$6.36 = 112.36$$

Simple interest is good, but compound interest is the best type of interest to make. The following table shows why that is:

Years Invested	Principal	Simple Interest (10%)	Compound Interest (10%)
1	$1,000	$1,100	$1,100.00
2		1,200	1,210.00
3		1,300	1,331.00
4		1,400	1,464.10
5		1,500	1,610.51
6		1,600	1,771.56
7		1,700	1,948.72
8		1,800	2,143.60
9		1,900	2,357.96
10		2,000	2,593.76
11		2,100	2,853.14
12		2,200	3,138.45
13		2,300	3,452.30
14		2,400	3,797.53
15		2,500	4,177.28
16		2,600	4,595.00
17		2,700	5,054.50
18		2,800	5,559.95
19		2,900	6,115.95
20		3,000	6,727.54

After twenty years, the amount earned through compound interest is more than double the total amount earned through simple interest!

PAY YOURSELF FIRST

Paying yourself first is the most important tool of the rich. This concept means that whenever you get some money, you pay yourself a minimum of 10 percent of that money before you pay anyone else.

You never pay yourself less than 10 percent. Ever. The money that you pay to yourself and save is to be used only for investing for the rest of your life; it's never to be spent on things. For some people, money simply passes through their lives. They get paid $500 and spend $500. Eventually these people can spend more than they make. If you make $500 each week, you have only earned for yourself what you decide to keep. If you decide not to pay yourself first, you may have an extra $50 to spend (10 percent of $500); however, this $50, if saved, could add up to thousands of dollars over time.

The pay-yourself-first rule applies to any money coming into your life. When you get a cash gift from a relative, you pay yourself first. When you find a $5 bill at the park, you pay yourself first. When you get your paycheck or a bonus, you pay yourself first. When you get your allowance, you pay yourself first.

When you pay yourself first, you put that money in a special account that you will learn about later in this chapter. You never touch this money; it is best to consider it to be locked in the vault or untouchable. If you do this, the money grows and grows and grows. Your money begins to work and creates more money, which itself works to create more money, and so on.

And this money isn't just to retire on. You will also want to use it as collateral when you conduct future business with financial institutions. If you have savings, they will take you seriously. If you don't have savings, they might deny you what you want.

SMALL AMOUNTS ADD UP!

Check out these examples to find out how much paying yourself first can pay off if you start early in life.

Scenario One

Start Age	**15**
End Age	65
Initial Deposit Amount	$10
Periodic Deposit Amount	$10
Deposit Frequency	Weekly
Annual Rate of Return	10%

Scenario One	
Total Deposits	$26,010
Growth	$609,596
Accumulated Value	*$635,606*

Scenario Two

Start Age	**20**
End Age	65
Initial Deposit Amount	$10
Periodic Deposit Amoun	$10
Deposit Frequency	Weekly
Annual rate of return	10%

Scenario Two	
Total Deposits	$23,410
Growth	$369,185
Accumulated Value	*$392,595*

Scenario Three

Start Age	**30**
End Age	65
Initial Deposit Amount	$10
Periodic Deposit Amount	$10
Deposit Frequency	Weekly
Annual rate of return	10%

Scenario Three	
Total Deposits	$18,210
Growth	$129,803
Accumulated Value	*$148,013*

Learning how to pay yourself first results in proven wealth creation. By skimming off the 10 percent, you build up money that is available for investment and financial growth. I promise you that you will not miss the money in your daily life, and you will eventually learn to appreciate what the money will do for you over the years when you become independently wealthy.

MY MONEY MANAGEMENT SYSTEM

In our Kids Ride to Riches seminars, we teach basic money management to kids. We've developed a system using account boxes that represent the six basic categories of saving. Using the account system combines an activity and a concept of how money needs to be spent. If done consistently over time, anyone can learn the habitual practice of saving money and designating it for the six different purposes. For the kids in our seminars, money management is a new concept. They rarely see their parents do it or talk about it. We give them a system that they can use to help them budget their money.

THE SIX ACCOUNTS

Each of the six money accounts has a name and a purpose, and it's your job to allocate your money into each account for a particular use. This is a money management system.

Most people don't manage their money because they're never taught to do so. Yet, the entire economic structure around us is based upon money management. For example, all companies must decide how to spend, where to spend, when to spend, when to sell, how to make profit, and then repeat the cycle. This is called money management or, in the business world, "capital management."

People are like mini companies; yet we don't have a corporate structure that helps us manage our money. Without money management, there's no way of telling how much you can spend, how to spend, where to spend, when to spend, and how to reach your financial goals, like buying a car or paying for university.

Saving money is the most important tool in shaping your financial future. Without savings, most people live day to day and are unprepared for emergencies or major life transitions, large expenditures, or a secure retirement.

Savings gives you the power to see ahead, just like a company sees ahead and creates strategies for its revenues and expenses. Knowing that you have savings gives you the assurance that you can afford what you want and that you will always have enough.

Account #1: Riches (10 percent)

This account is for savings for riches. Here is where you invest the pay-yourself-first amount so it can grow for your future. This is the most important account because the money that you deposit into this account will make you more and more money. This money is regularly invested so it can earn interest. Over time this will reinforce your understanding of the time value of money.

Account #2: Expenses (50 percent)

This account is for your monthly expenses and covers what you need to live each month, including everyday necessities. Adults and families have to pay rent or a house payment, water, electricity, gas, telephone, cable television or satellite television, food, clothing, and car expenses every month. Those expenses usually amount to about 50 percent of the money that you get in each paycheck. Sometimes it can be more than that, but 50 percent is a good amount to budget for your bills.

Account #3: Savings (10 percent)

This account is for the 10 percent of your income that you save to spend later. You use the money in this account to pay for items that you really need or want to buy, such as a bike, car, etc. It can also be used for unplanned circumstances and emergencies. This account can be subdivided into multiple smaller accounts depending on what you're saving for.

Account #4: Education (10 percent)

This account is for money for technical school, college, and university— or lifelong learning opportunities, such as seminars, conferences, and courses. Even after you have completed your secondary education, you will maintain an education account and it will be used for lifelong learning.

Account #5: Fun (10 percent)

This account is for money that you will spend every month on fun things, like movies, concert tickets, clothes, and trendy items like accessories or technology that you don't really need but really, really want. Spend this money every month no matter what. Have fun with your fun account. This account balances the other savings accounts and is a way for you to have fun with your money. This is your reward!

Account #6: Giving (5–10 percent)

This account is for donations, charity, and other forms of giving. You may want to donate to the local food bank or send your money to a developing nation or help cats and dogs at your local animal shelter. Whatever your cause, the giving account is based on the principle of abundance. Whatever you give freely, you will receive freely in return. We live in a richer and more satisfying world when we help others along the way. Others have helped you at times, and it's your turn to return the kindness to someone else. We are meant to help each other. I believe that we become that much richer by helping others become wealthy as well. There is plenty to go around. We live in an abundant world.

PRACTICING MONEY MANAGEMENT

Just like learning anything new, such as dancing or sports, you have to practice basic money management before you get really good at it. After twenty-one days of consistent practice, something becomes a habit that you will continue. During those first twenty-one days of using the money account boxes, the kids who take our seminars need coaching and encouragement at home. Support from parents helps the child succeed.

I encourage you to use the money in each account for its designated purpose. Enjoy spending the money for what you really want and need. I think the most enjoyment is in knowing that when you stay with this habit of money management, you will not only have fun spending your budgeted money, you will also enjoy having your money work for you while you're having fun. You will begin to notice how your friends who don't use a money management system struggle, probably spending everything they earn.

Mismanaged money has a price that is too high to pay. Money management can be enjoyable and satisfying. You can accumulate wealth *and* be secure in your future by paying yourself first (10 percent) and managing the remainder (90 percent).

FAMILY SUCCESS CHECKLIST

$ Pay yourself first—no matter what!

$ Invest 10 percent of your income and let these savings work for you.

$ Get into the habit of saving for riches.

$ Using the six accounts enables you to stay on track.

$ Use the money that you have allotted for each month's spending.

$ At the end of each month, go over your expenses and check your savings progress.

$ Stay with your money management plan for at least three months. You will form a good habit.

PART II

LET'S DO... BECOME A RICHER YOU

50 and 100 suite apartment buildings built by Doug Meharg in the '60s and '70s.

Skyloft Ski and Country Club New Lodge, built in the late '90s.

CHAPTER 10

MAKE YOUR MONEY WORK FOR YOU

"We go to school to learn to work hard for money.
I write books and create products that teach people
how to have money work hard for them."

—ROBERT KIYOSAKI

We touched on the difference between how the rich think and how the poor think.

Most people work to pay the bills and don't think beyond that. They might dream occasionally and say, "When I get a raise, things will be better" or "When I start my new job, things will be better" or "When we get the kids through college, then we can ..." People who live this way are always dreaming about something that will never happen. Why? Because they believe good things will happen, but it's always sometime in the future. They don't realize that with that kind of mind-set they are limiting themselves to never quite making it to their goal. With no PERMA goal, no visualization, no perseverance, and no system, they don't cross the finish line.

Some people use affirmations to change their way of thinking. It can definitely be a part of your success. We talked some about affirmations earlier. Focusing on the positive and putting statements in present tense makes your subconscious work on the belief process. If you're going to dream, don't limit yourself by saying "when …." Another mistake we make is to say, "If I could just get the support I need to …" or "If I could have what I need, then I would …." The words *if, when, but,* and *can't* aren't used by successful and wealthy people. How often do you use those words without even thinking about the limitations you put on yourself?

The average poor or middle-class family lives in a paradigm that only sees what is inside the box. There's nothing wrong with working for someone else and doing an honest day's work for an honest day's pay if that's what you *truly want to do*. I want to offer an alternative to everyone who wants to know how to create a better life for herself and teach her children how to have a better life. Every parent wants her child to grow up healthy, happy, and in a better circumstance than she did. If we don't teach our children the skills it takes to be successful, then they will be stuck in the same box.

You've decided to take the steps as a family to learn money management, saving, investing, and letting money work for you. When your children grow up and have families, they will pass on the valuable lessons that used to be available only to the rich.

Poor and average people work because they feel they have to work to survive. They don't save because they don't think they can afford to. In reality, they can't afford not to save for the future. You won't miss the 10 percent you pay yourself, and before long that invested money will be working for you and multiplying your income. The wealthy work because they want to or enjoy it. They use money as a tool to make more money that enables them to be who they want to be and do what they want to do. Some of you may not like the idea of making money for yourself without helping others, too. Many wealthy people spend a large percentage of their money on good causes and foundations that help with medical and social problems both in Canada and around the world.

Money makes you independent. You can enjoy yourself without worrying about money. I'm not saying that money is the answer to every problem, but it can certainly help take care of the needs of you, your family, and others. I believe that part of the real satisfaction in life comes from helping other people, which is one of the reasons I founded Kids Ride to Riches and wrote this book.

THE WINNING STRATEGY

You have to learn the winning strategy and then make it your own. We've talked about the great things that you learn from playing games to understand the strategies and money management skills. Think about Monopoly for a minute. The key is to buy property, develop four green houses, and then turn those into a hotel.

It's a lesson in managing the money you have and a strategy for investing.

Rich people know they must have their money working for them, instead of working for money. This means they invest their riches account in opportunities that offer them a rate of return usually greater than 4 percent interest. A good rate of return to achieve is 10 percent.

Their money is invested to grow and make more money, which in turn is reinvested to make more money. When this happens on a big scale, rich people spend their time researching investments and finding new opportunities to grow their money, rather than working for money themselves.

There are many types of investments, and these are the four most common:

BONDS	A bond is an IOU certifying that you loaned money to a government or corporation and outlines the terms of repayment. A buyer may purchase bonds at a discount. The bond has a fixed interest rate for a fixed period of time. When the time is up, the bond is said to have "matured," and the buyer may redeem the bond for the full face value. Investors do not have access to their money as easily when they invest in bonds. Bonds can be corporate (sold by private companies to raise cash); municipal (issued by nonfederal governments); and federal (issued by the federal government; this is the lowest risk type of bond).

MUTUAL FUNDS	These are professionally managed portfolios made up of stocks, bonds, and other investments. Individuals buy shares in the fund, which in turn purchases stocks, bonds, and other investments. This system allows small investors to take advantage of professional account management and diversification normally available only to large investors. Types of mutual funds include balanced fund; global bond fund; growth fund; income fund; and regional stock funds, among many others.
STOCKS	These represent ownership of a corporation. Stockholders own a share of a company and are entitled to a share of the profits, as well as a vote in how the company is run. Company profits may be divided among all shareholders in the form of a dividend. Dividends are usually paid quarterly. Larger profits are made when the stock gains value in the open market. This gain (or loss!) is tracked in stock markets, like the Toronto Stock Exchange and the New York Stock Exchange. Stocks allow investors to have easy access to their money.

REAL ESTATE	This is property that is purchased and held as a long-term investment or purchased and sold for short-term gains. Real estate markets have a profit cycle, and it is important to buy low and sell higher. This is not always the case for stocks! Real estate offers excellent protection for investors against inflation, but it may be difficult to convert real estate to cash quickly. There is a time-delay with real estate investments.

I've built apartment buildings, houses, and a ski resort over the years. My real estate company sold for a good profit, and I invested that into a ski resort. I built up the ski resort and several years later sold it at a profit. All of this started when I was a teenager and built my first house. It was for family, as was the second. Then I decided I was really good at this and could make money doing it for others. After that, I learned that I could make more money and create more streams of income if I didn't have to do all the work myself. Do you see how this goes back to the same principle as playing Monopoly?

A key strategy to creating wealth is working to build assets, like a house or a business. Over time, your asset will be worth more than it was to begin with. With the increase in its value, you can later sell it for a larger profit. Selling a business can give you millions of dollars. After you have one asset built up, begin working on another. That is how you end up with several sources of income. It seems that most businesses start over a cup of coffee at a kitchen table. It just takes an idea and a dream. Yes, you will work hard while you build up your assets, but that just starts the whole thing moving. Soon your money will start working for you.

Many people don't actually have a plan for what to do with their riches account when it has grown to a substantive size (more than $1,000). It's fine to save money for something specific like a new stereo system, an LCD flat-screen television, or a trip to the Bahamas, but after you've accomplished that dream—then what?

Let's look at a bigger picture. You want to have your money work for you. In my life, I made much of my money in real estate. The way I choose to invest my riches account is to buy real estate that will increase in value through improvements over time. Then I sell it at a profit.

The money that you make from your investments, businesses, and real estate is always redirected into your riches account so your money is making more and more money. After you have a good cycle of money being invested, you may be pleasantly surprised at how quickly your riches account grows—and therefore, your net worth. And all because you implemented the money management system.

Most of the time, I invest my money in land that is in an area where there will be future development. If my town is growing on the west side, that's where I would invest in land. I don't buy the most expensive land, but rather land that is a little farther out of town for a cheaper price. Then, as development gets closer to the land, I sell it for top dollar, build houses to rent on it, or build a business park and rent out those spaces. Each of these is a good way to manage the land and the investment.

Before I invest in land and houses, I research the community's potential growth and what the future looks like. I encourage you to do the same in order to increase your knowledge about real estate investing. Use the decision-making skills we discussed to help you make the best decision.

FAMILY SUCCESS CHECKLIST

$ Learn about investing.

$ Understand the four main investment vehicles.

$ Prepare to invest your riches account money into an investment vehicle of your choice.

$ Set up your life so your money works for you twenty-four hours a day, seven days a week.

CHAPTER 11

BECOME A RICHER YOU

"Every human being has been 'born rich;' it's just that most people are temporarily a little short of money!"

—BOB PROCTOR, *YOU WERE BORN RICH*

You were born with an inner wealth that you may not be aware of … yet. Part of your wealth is made up of things. Part of your wealth is made up of things that you cannot see or hold.

Mark Victor Hansen and Robert G. Allen wrote *Cracking the Millionaire Code*. In it, they talk about wealth being made up of tangibles and intangibles. They say that people will be happier, more productive, and much more successful if we shift our focus away from external tangible assets—such as cars, clothes, and houses—toward internal intangible assets—such as happiness, joy, and love. What a powerful message.

Harvard Business School conducted a study about assets found in businesses and what types of assets they were. The researchers found that 75 percent of the assets in most major corporations are intangible, such as human capital, organization capital, information capital, culture capital, leadership capital, brand value, and customer loyalty. The intangibles produce the circumstances in which the corporation will make money. Hansen and Allen state that you can't have external wealth without internal wealth.

We've talked about the abundant world we live in, and I want you to go a step further and apply that to yourself—your personal assets. These personal assets are the same ones that were listed for corporations. Let me explain. You have personal human capital. You have talents and natural abilities that you were born with and those that you can develop. For example, right-brain talents could be your ability to design graphic arts, create sculpture, paint, or write. These are just a few assets. You won't possess them all, but you will have some that are specifically yours. Your left-brain assets would include your ability to learn and retain information. You may not have thought about it before, but you are an expert at something.

You are an example to others—when you succeed and when you don't. Your children watch everything you do and say. In business, it is the same. Others in your organization learn from your knowledge and your behaviour. You may use your knowledge to develop new and more innovative things that will make a better world. Using your six mental faculties enables you to tap into your inner wealth.

Your reputation, integrity, and honesty are assets that will put you in the position to develop good relationships, both personally and professionally. Every organization, including families, has what is called a culture. Simply put, culture is most easily recognized as what you think, what you say, and what you do. Whether you are negative or positive is reflected in your family culture. Your children will either copy your behaviour or will decide to be another way. Either way, each family member influences the culture.

There is some controversy over whether people are natural-born leaders. Your natural leadership skills are part of your inner wealth. If you learn quickly and then apply those new skills to your life, that is another asset. Your intelligence is an asset. I don't just mean people who have a high IQ. There are different types of intelligence, and all of them are part of your inner wealth.

Using all of these examples may have prompted you to create a list of your assets. Keep your list and refer to it as you move closer to achieving your goals of becoming a richer you. These assets are part of your wealth. Remember to cultivate them and add more to your list in the coming years.

THE LAW OF ATTRACTION REVISITED

Words and thoughts have power. If you don't think so, then look around yourself again. What kind of results are you getting right now? Are you getting what you say you want? If not, then you must not believe what you're saying. Just saying a positive affirmation won't change anything if you don't believe it. You end up sending out negative energy, and that is exactly what you get back according to the Law of Attraction. You need to make a conscious effort to change the message (energy) you are sending. It needs to be in your head as well as your heart. Beliefs are full of passion and direction. The feelings you have and show to others are an indication of the energy you are projecting and attracting. Do you want different results than you're experiencing right now? Then you know what to do!

You were born rich and meant to live a wealthy life that allows you to make the world a better place. No one is born to become poor and struggling. We are born into a world that is full of options and opportunities. The more obstacles you turn into opportunities, the richer you become.

Michael Losier, author of the *Law of Attraction*, says it best:

"When you go from what you don't want to what you do want, the words change. When the words change, the vibration changes, and you can only send out one vibration at a time."

This is one of my favorite quotes. It makes sense and explains why sometimes you can get mixed results. Losier explains that you have to reset your energy. You can instantly know if you are feeling confusion—negative or positive vibrations. You can almost throw a switch in your conscious mind to change from one to the other. It only takes a moment. You simply change the words you are using to switch from negative to positive. This changes the energy you are putting out and, therefore, changes the type of energy you are attracting back to yourself. The Law of Attraction is always at work. It doesn't remember the negative energy you were sending off a minute ago. It aligns with the positive energy you're giving off now. *It always responds to the present.* Practice being consistent and sending out positive energy so you get more of it in return.

LEARNING TO ALLOW

Part of accessing the riches you were born with is to mentally and emotionally allow yourself to be successful and achieve the goals you've set for yourself. This reinforces how important your self-image and your thoughts and beliefs are. Set up positive, self-fulfilling prophesies for yourself, rather than negative ones. Most of us find it challenging to realize that we are born with great potential.

ASKING PERMISSION

For some reason, many adults still think they need to have permission to do something. As a parent, you know that is one of the things you teach your children from the beginning. They need your permission to do something or go somewhere. When they are young, it's for their own safety. However, when you become an adult, you need to make the transition to being responsible for yourself and your actions.

You don't need anyone else's permission but your own to become a richer you. You can increase your possibilities just by taking that step. You can use your practical skills and become even stronger by focusing your attention on the goal. Following the tips and strategies in these pages will help you tap into your inner power.

When you allow new thoughts and experiences into your life, you increase the results that you receive through the Law of Attraction. You're able to be more creative and move past any limitations that held you back from succeeding.

Michael Losier states that we all have a bubble around us that is made up of the vibrational energy we create with our thoughts. It attracts people and things that respond to our energy. Who you are attracts a response. What do you want to attract?

Let me explain it this way. You are in a fenced-in yard. It's small, but there's a gate that you can open when you want to and close when you want to. The decision is up to you. What is inside the fence with you—inside your yard—is what you have already allowed into your life—friends, family, wealth, investments, and your material possessions. These things are already yours. The things you still desire are on the other side of the fence for now. To open the gate more often—to allow more often—is a conscious effort of putting out positive energy. Be deliberate and specific in your thoughts and actions. This gives you focus on bringing that thing you desire inside the fence with you. You open the gate and allow it to come into your life.

Being rich isn't limited to the small percentage of the population that was born into a wealthy family. You now know that we are all born rich with the capacity to allow prosperous things to happen to us.

FAMILY SUCCESS CHECKLIST

$ You were born rich.

$ You have inner wealth.

$ Your thoughts are the foundation for living the life you want.

$ A key to being rich is to allow yourself to be rich.

$ Allow money and other things into your life.

$ Be aware of how you make decisions and focus on using your thoughts to direct your results.

$ You don't have to understand everything about how the Law of Attraction works in order for it to work positively in your life.

Photo by Lindsay Green.

Skyloft Ski and Country Club chairlift, and local deer enjoying some off-season roaming.

CHAPTER 12

ROLL UP YOUR SLEEVES

"The size of your success is measured by the strength of your desire, the size of your dream, and how you handle disappointment along the way."

—ROBERT KIYOSAKI

The next step to becoming a richer you is to put the how to's that you learned in the first part of this book into action. The rest of this book contains the learning activities that help you and your family practice the skills you need to attain even higher levels of success—together!

ADVICE FOR PARENTS

Have you ever noticed that your children respond to learning something from people other than you sometimes? Do you and your child or teenager get frustrated with each other when you try to help him with his homework?

One of the reasons I advocate making the learning process fun is to avoid resistance—from you or your kids. We resist things we don't want to do. We learn when we're having fun without realizing it. What you and your children learn in games like Monopoly, Cashflow, Risk, and Pictionary are the principles of life skills.

You get to practice without any heavy penalties. It's only a game. Then you knowingly apply some of the things learned in the game to real life. Parents, it's your responsibility to encourage and help your kids make the application in daily life. Eventually, when your kids are living on their own, they will have the skills they need to be successful in whatever they choose to do.

Earlier we discussed that all of us are individuals and learn in different ways. Let's review some valuable information about working with different types of learners. Decide what type of learner you are and then try to understand your family's learning competencies. If you have two kids, they probably are not the same type of learner. They could be, but many times they aren't, so you have to know how to reach them both with the same message.

All of us learn better in the style with which we are the most comfortable. There are three main learning styles—visual, auditory, and kinesthetic. People who think in pictures and like to see diagrams and charts are visual learners. Auditory learners respond to sounds and speech. Kinesthetic learners like to get involved in activities and don't usually read directions. It is easier to work with visual and auditory types at the same time. For example, if you have a set of directions for a game or activity, you can see them as well as read them out loud. Role playing and games really appeal to the kinesthetic learner. Everyone has a little bit of each learning type inside them; however, there is often a dominant style that you will be able to easily identify in yourself and your family members.

Following this chapter is a series of activities that you can do to practice the ideas in the first part of *Become a Richer You*. The activities bring the words on these pages to life. I challenge you to do the activities. Remember what I said in the Introduction? Most people will not do the activities. Are you most people?

CONCLUSION

For you to get the most from this book, your whole family must be involved, especially parents. Involve your kids in the conversation about money. Start with scheduling family time twice a month specifically for this purpose. Make it an evening of fun, learning, and perhaps a bit of competition with each other.

As time passes, the opportunity for building skills is lost forever. If you take the time to have your kids in all kinds of other activities like hockey, computers, and soccer, perhaps money management can be included as a life skill, too. You will be glad that you spent the time to talk about creating riches. Your kids will thank you forever.

May you *Become a Richer You!*

ACTIVITY

THE "I CAN" ATTITUDE

I recommend that you do this activity as a family. Each person should have his own copy of the questions and be able to write his own answers. Then, share your results and help each other as needed in developing these lists. This activity helps you identify self-limiting beliefs and empowering beliefs that you have as individuals and as a family.

Use the following guidelines to help you. Begin by looking at limiting beliefs. Then look at self-empowering beliefs. If you need more room than what is provided, get a notebook that you can use for all the activities in this book. I suggest that each family member have his own notebook.

Spend some time completing and discussing this activity as a family. The exercise has three parts, so you can focus on one part at a time and spread the activity out over a few evenings.

PART I

1. List beliefs you have about yourself that limit you.
   For example:

   I won't …

   I can't …

   I never …

   I don't like …

2. List beliefs that your family shares that limit your family success (money, time, health, fun, spirit/religion, education, etc.). For example:

   We never go …

   We never have enough …

   We don't believe …

   We can't ever …

3. Go over your answers for question #1 and turn them into "I can" or positive statements. Refer back in the chapter about how to do this if you need to.

4. Go over your answers for question #2 and turn them into "we can" or positive statements.

PART II:

1. List positive beliefs you have about yourself. For example:

    I can …

    I love …

    I have …

    I am …

2. List positive beliefs you have about your family. For example:

    We always have …

    We feel that …

    We are good at …

    We love …

PART III

1. Now create some positive statements about yourself that are new and different by using the "I can" system. Post these in your room or on a mirror, or put one in your wallet where you will see it. For example:

    "I can save money because now I know the money management system."

    "I can get great grades in school because I say so!"

2. Now create some positive statements about your family that are new and different using the "I can" system. You could post them on a family bulletin board or on the refrigerator so the whole family can see them every day. For example:

"We can talk about money together."

"We can set goals as a family and achieve them together."

ACTIVITY

MOVIE NIGHT

Pick one of your family's favorite movies and watch it together with popcorn and drinks. Depending on the age of your kids, some movie options are:

Kids under age eight
The Sound of Music

Kids ages eight to ten
The Wizard of Oz

Preteens and Teens
The Titans
We Are Marshall

You could use other types of movies, but sports-themed movies are good ones in which to see examples of attitudes and beliefs. Most of these movies feature an underdog that goes through challenges to overcome adversity and becomes a winner.

I encourage you and your family to discuss attitudes, successes, challenges, failures, and the end results.

Use the following questions in your discussion:

1. How can you learn from these characters and their attitudes?

2. Did their attitudes change through the story? How?

3. What happened to help them decide to go after their goals and dreams?

4. How did the attitudes of each person or team member affect the rest of the team?

5. What qualities of the coach/parent worked well to encourage and build up the team's success rate?

6. What did the coach do that didn't work? Why didn't it work?

7. What kind of reaction did the characters have when they failed? What did they do about it?

8. What was the final result?

9. What key thing did they say or do that made the most difference in their results?

10. Which character in the movie inspired you? Why?

ACTIVITY

THE LAW OF ATTRACTION

The following activities will help you and your family better understand the Law of Attraction.

MOVIE NIGHT:

Watch the movie *The Secret* as a family. Discuss the Law of Attraction and what you learned from the film.

Answer these questions together:

1. How does the Law of Attraction work?

2. Have you ever concentrated on what you don't want rather than what you do want? In what circumstances did you do this?

3. Have you ever used the Law of Attraction to get something?

4. How could you use the Law of Attraction to get something?

5. What do you personally want to attract?

6. What do you want to attract as a family?

WHAT DO YOU WANT?

This is a key question to ask yourself and your family. Write down what you want and be specific. This list can be as short or as long as you want, but don't make it look like a shopping list or a wish list of stuff—what Robert Kiyosaki refers to as doo-dads.

Come up with key, important things you want. You will attract the people who resonate to that focus. Discuss these as a family and help each other be clear in your statements.

Test it out! Focus on a short-term thing you want and be passionate about feeling, tasting, seeing, hearing, and enjoying exactly what you want.

Remember, if you send out several thoughts at the same time for different things, it doesn't work as well. When you concentrate on one thing at a time, you send out focused energy, and there is clarity in what you are attracting.

See what happens. Then move on to the next item you want to focus on.

KEEP A LAW OF ATTRACTION JOURNAL

My daughter keeps a Law of Attraction Journal, and I encourage you to do the same. Write down every time you notice the Law of Attraction working in your life. My daughter records small things and big things— such as receiving the book that she wanted to read and finding the perfect real estate deal she wanted to hear about.

This is a powerful tool because it does two things: (1.) It creates a *track record* of your ability to use the Law of Attraction and manifest things in your life; and (2.) Whatever you focus on increases. As you notice the Law of Attraction at work in your life, it will work more and more often.

KEEP A GRATITUDE JOURNAL

Every day, take one minute and experience gratitude for what you already have. Be grateful for love, relationships, time, money, spirit, health, your home, your apartment, your car, your clothes, and all the things that are a part of your life now. If you are grateful for what you have now, the universe will help you have even more so that you are more and more grateful.

An example entry could be: I felt grateful today at school when a friend offered to share his lunch with me because I forgot my own; or, I am so happy and grateful that I found the exact car I wanted to buy with a $3,000 rebate.

ACTIVITY

INNER-WEALTH EVALUATION SURVEY

You can do this survey on your own, but I suggest that you do it as a family activity. Each person can answer the questions individually and then you can share and discuss them. Another way is to go through and answer them aloud, giving each person a chance to give her answer. A third suggestion is to complete the survey in your individual notebooks.

Sometimes it is difficult to realize what your own assets are. This is not a time to be shy or self-conscious. Help each other discover your true inner assets and inner wealth. The first five categories will be easier for family members of high school age and adults. However, I've included five revised categories that can be used more easily with younger children or preteens. This way your whole family can participate.

Make a list of your assets for each category in the space available. Remember these are not physical tangible assets, but intangible assets.

1. Personal assets: Characteristics (i.e. perseverance, integrity, honesty)

2. Personal assets: Talents (i.e. specific artistic abilities, writing, good with numbers)

3. Personal information assets: What are you knowledgeable about? (You may be an expert in this field, i.e. computer programming, data entry, accounting, libraries)

4. Personal leadership qualities or experience (be specific)

5. Personal organizational skills (be specific)

CATEGORIES FOR YOUNGER CHILDREN

1. Personal characteristics. (List qualities that you have. Ask your mom or dad for help if you need it. Include things like you are honest, helpful, etc.)

2. Personal talents. (List your talents or things you like to do. Include things like you are good at reading, dance, playing an instrument, etc.)

3. Personal information. (List things you've learned and things you are interested in learning more about.)

4. Personal experience—leadership. (List any activities you are involved in where you are a leader or are learning leadership skills.)

5. Personal experience—organization skills. (List any activities at school or home where you are demonstrating or practicing organizational skills.)

ACTIVITY

DISCOVERING RICHES

This activity is a research and share project. Challenge your children to pick someone who is wealthy. Each child can pick a different person. You have to pick a person, too.

Look up the person on the Internet and find out everything you can about that person's life and what they have done in business. Some suggestions are Andrew Carnegie, Bill and Melinda Gates, and Oprah Winfrey. You may be interested in finding out about other people.

Some people who are wealthy inherited their fortunes, but many people have come up from meager beginnings. Even those who inherited wealth had to learn to manage their money. Some may have suffered failures along the way and built up a new business and become very successful again. Find out how they built up their wealth and what their childhood was like. Share the information over your favorite dinner and discuss the lessons you can learn from these successful businesspeople.

Compare the lessons you're reading in this book to what you learn about them.

ACTIVITY

MONEY MANAGEMENT

Play Monopoly

Monopoly can help children of all ages learn something about managing money. The game doesn't have a savings account as part of the game, but you could add that to the game to help your kids understand the concept and what can happen when you learn to save and invest intelligently.

Play Cashflow and Cashflow for Kids

Robert Kiyosaki created these two games to show people how to manage their money and get out of the rat race. Thanks, Robert! These games are awesome learning tools for adults and kids. My daughter and son-in-law continue to play Cashflow because they learn from it every time they play. Robert says that how you play Cashflow is how you manage money in life. Try it and see.

ACTIVITY

PERSONAL GOALS: WHAT DO YOU WANT?

You've learned a lot about goal setting and what part it plays in becoming a success. This activity helps you set personal goals. Each family member can do this activity individually. Visit our website www.kidsridetoriches.com to download additional copies of Kids Ride to Riches Personal Goal Sheets for your whole family. Complete new goal sheets every few months.

After everyone has completed their personal goal sheets, have a family show-and-tell where everyone can describe their personal goals to one another.

Start with one or two major goals—perhaps financial goals—and use the personal goal sheets to outline these goals. Eventually, you can have more than one or two major goals after you get good at setting and achieving your goals.

Have a family discussion at the three-month, six-month, and one-year markers. Remember to collectively celebrate the achievement of your goals!

GOAL-SETTING TIPS

The most successful goal statements have the following elements: *present tense, emotional, realistic, measurable,* and *action-based.* And that spells PERMA, which is short for *permanent.*

Present tense

Emotional

Realistic

Measurable

Action-based

Personal Goals

The best goals are *present tense, emotional, realistic, measurable,* and *action-based:*

PERMA

Goal	Completion Date

Setting and achieving goals is a proven wealth-creation tool!

ACTIVITY

FAMILY GOALS

After you have all completed your personal goal sheets, it's time to create family goals. These are goals that your family wants to complete together. Good examples are riding in a bikeathon; collecting a certain amount of money for a charity; volunteering as a family for a worthy community cause; or planning and going on a family vacation.

After you've completed the forms and discussed the goals and how they will be reached with your kids, post the family goal sheet on a family bulletin board or the fridge so you can encourage each other along the way. Visit our website www.kidsridetoriches.com to download additional copies of Kids Ride to Riches family goal sheets. Complete new family goal sheets every few months.

Remember to collectively celebrate the achievement of your goals!

GOAL-SETTING TIPS

As you know, most successful goal statements have the following elements: *present tense, emotional, realistic, measurable,* and *action-based.* And that spells PERMA, which is short for *permanent.*

Present tense

Emotional

Realistic

Measurable

Action-based

Family Goals

The best goals are *present tense, emotional, realistic, measurable,* and *action-based:*
PERMA

Goal	Completion Date

Setting and achieving goals is a proven wealth-creation tool!

ACTIVITY

OVERCOMING OBSTACLES ON THE ROAD TOWARD YOUR GOALS

What obstacles are in your way? What obstacles are stopping your family from achieving success? This activity helps you discuss obstacles and brainstorm creative ways of overcoming them on the road to achieving your goals.

Answer these questions:

1. What is stopping me from becoming richer?

2. What is stopping our family from becoming richer?

3. In what way could these obstacles be eliminated?
    (Be creative!)

4. How would their elimination cause me to become
    a richer me/us sooner?

ACTIVITY

POSITIVE COMPETITION

Post a chart on the refrigerator or a family bulletin board with each person's name over a column.

Each time you hear someone say a negative statement beginning with *don't, not, no,* or *never,* put a mark under his name.

See who has the fewest number of marks at the end of the week. Have fun with this. Kids especially like catching their parents at this.

ACTIVITY

PICTIONARY

This is a great game to understand the relationship between words and pictures. You can do a variation on the game by choosing words or terms used in this book.

Word List: Money

Investment

Budget

Dream

Savings account

Money management

The Law of Attraction

Vibration or vibes

Encourage the whole family to glance back through the book—including the glossary at the end of the book—and your other Kids Ride to Riches materials for words or terms to include in the game.

ACTIVITY

RICHES FIELD TRIPS

Field trips are some of the best ways to learn how the real world works and see how successful businesses operate. Let your children be a part of the planning and help choose where to visit. If you have more than one child, you can take each of them to a specific type of business and talk with them about what they do. Some communities have business mentor programs for high school-age students. They learn from businessmen and women what goes on in the real world of business.

THE BANK

If your child doesn't have a savings account, then open one. Let them talk to the account representative with your guidance. Make arrangements beforehand or go at a time when the staff is not very busy. Your child can talk to a teller, customer assistant, and maybe a loan officer. She will begin to learn what these staff do and how the bank works. The staff can explain how checking and savings accounts work, how to make deposits and withdrawals, and what the interest rates are for saving and borrowing money. A loan officer could briefly explain the process of applying for a loan, how it works, and what types of loans the bank makes. Ask questions about the differences and similarities of credit cards and debit cards. Encourage your child to take a notebook so she can take notes about what she learns.

After you're finished at the bank, discuss what your child learned and answer any questions that she may have. Go through interest rates, payments required, and any other information that she needs to know.

THE GROCERY STORE

A visit to the grocery store doesn't have to be a scheduled field trip. Take advantage of your regular shopping trip to reinforce the money management skills your children learned in earlier chapters of this book.

Show them how to get the best value for their money while shopping for food. Show them how to compare products and pricing. Help them learn to get quality food without paying premium prices. It will help them learn about the relationship between quality and pricing. If they have helped with the menu, let them do the shopping with your guidance.

A great lesson to teach them at the grocery store is one that many adults aren't aware of. Look at the posted price labels for each product. Compare unit prices. Look at the amount per ounce or unit measure for the package or container. For example, one 32-ounce product could cost less per ounce than a 16-ounce container. Sometimes it's better to purchase the more expensive brand if the quality is much better. Explain your reasoning and decisions to your children.

When you go to purchase the groceries, encourage your kids to watch as the items are scanned by the cashier. Then let them make the transaction so they can learn the concept of value and exchange.

Older children are more familiar with value and exchange, but it's helpful for them to know the costs of household goods and necessities before they leave home to live on their own.

THE REAL ESTATE OFFICE

Make arrangements to go to a real estate office and meet with one of the agents. It might be best to call ahead so an agent can block out some time for you and your children. Explain to the agent that you are on a family field trip and what types of information you want them to share with your children. Be sure you allow time for questions from the children so they can understand the information they have been given.

A discussion about purchasing a home is the best place to begin. Have the agent go through the steps in the process, a hypothetical purchase, the basics of the required paperwork, mortgages, closing fees, property taxes, and real estate agent commissions/fees. The explanation doesn't have to be too detailed, but it does need to cover the entire process so your kids understand it and have the information they'll require when the time comes for them to buy real estate.

THE CAR DEALERSHIP

If you have a teenager who is approaching driving age or has just passed his driver's test, then he will really enjoy this trip. It could be a way of finding out what kinds of vehicles are available for future reference.

This could be a field trip, or if you are in the market for a new car, take your child with you. Let him be in on all the steps of the process. Look at new as well as used cars. This is another good way for him to learn value and exchange. The credit or loan officer who discusses the actual purchase and its terms can also tell your child how important it is to establish and maintain good credit.

The finance manager will probably be glad to share stories, without names of course, of people who have qualified for car loans or not. Your child can also learn whether it is better to finance a major purchase or pay cash.

THE INVESTMENT OR BROKERAGE FIRM

If you use a brokerage firm to manage your investments, make arrangements with your broker to bring along your child when your broker has some time to spend with you.

Let your broker know what you want your child to learn—different types of investments, rates of return, and what that means. Many adults don't understand the difference between corporate stocks and mutual funds. Ask about bonds and commodities. You don't have to get too deep into all the details of investments, but it is good for your child to learn the basics.

If you have a teenager, arrange for her to open an account, do the paperwork with the broker, and decide what investment to make. It is best if you let your teenager set up an account with a small amount of money. This is a learning process. Big investments are for later.

ACTIVITY

OVERCOMING OBSTACLES:
CELEBRATE FAMILY VICTORIES!

Decide on a prize that your kids and teens can earn for overcoming obstacles at school or work. When they do well at applying the lessons about overcoming obstacles, be sure you celebrate.

Each time a child succeeds, he needs to be rewarded. Have a special night out or a free pass for no chores on a weekend. You can create incentives and rewards as a family that inspire each of you to meet challenges head-on and overcome them.

WEEKEND TRIP OR OUTING

Help your teenagers and their younger siblings to plan a weekend trip or outing to somewhere the whole family is excited about going. You can use the account boxes to finance the trip. Let the kids do all the planning under your guidance. Try not to interfere with what they want to do as long as it is not a safety issue. It helps them use their financial management skills and their decision and planning skills. Supply maps and any other information they need.

PLAY THE GAME RISK

Risk is a board game that involves decision making, seeing the whole picture, making alliances with other players, and overcoming what look like obstacles to winning the game. As the title suggests, it also involves deciding which risks to take and then taking them. It is a fun way of practicing some of the skills we've discuss in this book.

ACTIVITY

THE MILLIONAIRE'S READING LIST

I've spent a lifetime creating a list of must-reads for gaining wealth, health, and happiness. These books are the best the industry has to offer and are authored by truly beautiful individuals. Some of the authors are no longer with us, while others are still thriving and making the world a better place.

The list I include here is the best place to begin your learning process with your family. I always feel overwhelmed when someone gives me a huge list of homework, so I've kept this list short on purpose.

Use these books and multimedia sources as touchstones for becoming a richer you!

BOOKS

Working with the Law by Raymond Holliwell

The Science of Getting Rich by Wallace T. Wattles

The One-Minute Millionaire by Mark Victor Hansen and Robert Allen

Think and Grow Rich by Napoleon Hill

MULTIMEDIA

Movie: *The Secret*

Audio: *The Strangest Secret* by Earl Nightingale

ACTIVITY

SIX MENTAL FACULTIES

These activities are a first step in building your mental muscles so you can use them in developing a prosperous future. Each mental faculty activity can be played as an age-appropriate game or as a family activity for parents and teenagers. I suggest that you only do one in an evening. Children and young people learn faster when they are having fun.

Perception: This is how you see yourself and the world around you. For younger children, discuss perception with them to be sure they understand what it is. Then together make a list of words that best describes each of you. Include two or three words for each family member. A parent, or child old enough to write, can record the list. Next cut out the words so one word appears on each slip of paper. Put the slips into a small paper bag or bowl and mix them up. Take turns pulling out a word slip. A parent or older child reads the word, and the family guesses who it is. I encourage you to have fun with this and get creative. This is a good opportunity to see what your children think of themselves and for you to reinforce positive words. Remember this is a game. Parents should not be judgmental about words the children think up.

For older children and teenagers, ten years and up, discuss the faculty and then ask each person to write down three to five words that describe the way he sees himself. When finished, each member of the family shares his list. This is not the time to try to fix any particular problem; it's meant to recognize what your preteen and teenager think. Do it over pizza or a favorite dessert and keep the discussion light and engaging.

Reasoning: Parents can begin by discussing that reasoning is simply how we think to figure things out. You can use games you already have around the house to demonstrate the activity. Choose a game that involves information or objects and a solution that they have to find. Some examples are Clue, Jenga, Guesstures, and Boggle. Remember that it needs to be age appropriate. I realize that our children and grandchildren play video and computer games, but I suggest staying away from those for this activity. One of the purposes of these activity sessions is to have personal interaction between parents and children or teens. During or after the game, have a conversation about how they used their reasoning to play the game. Have fun and teach your children and young adults how to think things through.

Memory: I'm sure every adult has heard that if you don't use it, you lose it. We have to exercise our memory throughout life. For **younger children,** several types of matching and memory games are available in stores. You and your child can make your own game by cutting out pictures from magazines and making a collage. Glue all of the pictures on a piece of poster board. Then look at the collage for 30–45 seconds. Turn the collage over and write down all the things that each of you remembers seeing. After you've finished the list, turn the collage over and see how you did.

For **preteens and teens,** you can encourage them by discussing a book they recently read or a magazine article about their favorite computer game and how it is rated. Or ask them what their favorite movie is and have them recall the plot, the main characters, and the actors. Let them help you with a topic for the conversation; just be sure you relate the use of the memory faculty as a part of the discussion. Again, a discussion over favorite family snacks works well for teens. Don't forget to keep it fun and short.

Intuition: The concept of intuition is difficult for a younger child to understand. They have intuition, but don't necessarily know what it is or how to use it. Briefly explain what intuition is using the description of this mental faculty from this chapter as a basis. If you make the explanation conversational and use your own words, they will better understand how it works. Tell a story or read a short story about a character who has good intuition. You could watch one of the Harry Potter movies and then discuss with your children how Harry and his friends use their intuition. Pick any movie that your children or teenagers enjoy watching that demonstrates this concept. Be sure to let them know that boys and girls have intuition.

Older children and teenagers have a pretty good grasp of what intuition is and the beliefs that our society has about intuition. Movies are good to share with teenagers to open up the discussion. It's very important when discussing intuition that older children understand its okay to trust their feelings. If they are in a situation where they feel threatened in some way, then they are most likely using their intuition. They need to listen to it and follow the promptings. One of the worst things children can experience is to have their feelings invalidated. I believe that is why many adults don't think they have access to intuition.

Will: Parents understand very well the strong-willed child. Unfortunately, we usually punish children for being stubborn and out of control when they exercise their willpower in a negative manner. Of course, we want to keep our children and young people from getting hurt or doing something that could cause consequences that they can't see. One of our goals as parents is to develop the mental faculty so your child or teenager can use it to accomplish goals. I suggest that you decide as a family to do a project that will take some effort but is age appropriate for your children. Be sure they have plenty of input into the decision. Maybe even let them decide what the project will be. If they are part of the decision-making process, then they will feel more involved in the activity, especially teenagers.

This shouldn't be a seasonal chore or something you've wanted to get done around the house, unless your teenager decides he wants to do that. This should be something fun. It could be a service project in your neighborhood or for an elderly person. The activity needs to have a challenge so that willpower and persistence play a part in the accomplishment. It could be participating in a walkathon or bicycle challenge. If you have teens and young children, then some activities may be done separately. Encourage your children to include some of their friends in the challenge activity. It is even more fun, and you teach your own children as well as others.

Imagination: This one can really be fun. Literally, the sky's the limit. You have as many options as you can think of—the bonus is that while you're thinking up ideas, you are using your imagination. Let me make some suggestions for activities you can use. **For younger children**, they could draw or paint a picture of what they want to be when they grow up. They could cut out pictures showing people doing what they want to do and make a personal collage that they could put up on their bedroom wall. Have them make up a story and either act it out with siblings or friends or write it down. If they write it down, they can then draw or cut out pictures to illustrate the story and make the whole thing into a small book. Craft books supply many ideas for children to create things. The process uses visualization of what they want it to look like and stimulates their imagination. These are just a few suggestions for you to do together and discuss how their imagination works.

For teenagers, you can use some of the same activities adjusted for age. Encourage them to write stories, draw, or create any other form of art that they are interested in. They may love music and compose something for their instrument or write lyrics. Supplies for making jewelry are easily available.

Discuss with your kids who they want to be and what they want in life. Encourage them to dream. In our Kids Ride to Riches program, we encourage families to go through this learning opportunity together. The activities in this book are only a glimpse of the full program that is offered through our programs, webinars, and teleseminars.

THE LANGUAGE OF MONEY

GLOSSARY OF TERMS

account: Money deposited with a financial institution for investment and/or safekeeping.

annual fee: A yearly fee charged to a customer to participate in an open-ended credit program.

annual percentage rate (APR): The cost of credit expressed as a yearly rate. APR is a percentage that results from an equation considering the amount financed, the finance charges, and the term of the loan.

assets: Items of monetary value (e.g., house, land, car) owned by an individual or a company.

ATM: Automated teller machine.

balance: An outstanding amount of money. In banking, balance refers to the amount of money in a particular account. In credit, balance refers to the amount owed.

balance transfer: Repayment of one credit debt with another credit source.

bank: An establishment for lending, issuing, borrowing, exchanging, and safeguarding money.

bankruptcy: A legal action taken when a credit holder cannot repay his or her debt. It modifies or eliminates the legal responsibility to repay some forms of debt. This is a serious action that can have serious consequences on a consumer's financial future.

billing cycle: The period of time that a credit statement covers.

billing statement: The summary of all actions applied to a credit account during a billing cycle. These can include payments, purchases, finances charges, fees, and other transactions.

bond: An IOU issued by a corporation, the government, or a city that is held by the lender as receipt that the business or institution has borrowed a specific amount of money. All bonds pay interest yearly and are payable in full at a specified date written on the bond.

bounced check: A check that a bank has refused to cash or pay because you have no funds in your account to cover the amount. This is also called NSF or insufficient funds.

cancelled check: A used check that has been paid and subtracted from the check writer's account. Cancelled checks have extra data on them from the bank. These can be requested from the bank, usually for a fee, or are available online.

capital: A stock of accumulated wealth used or available for producing more wealth.

cardholder agreement: The written statement that defines and explains all legal terms for a credit card agreement. It includes payment terms, billing dispute procedures, and communications guidelines, among other items.

cash: Money in the form of paper and coins. In banking, this is the act of paying a check.

charge card: A card that requires a user to pay off the entire balance every month.

check: Any written document instructing a bank to pay money from the writer's account.

checking account: An account for which the holder can write checks. Checking accounts pay less interest than savings accounts, or none at all.

clear: A check clears when its amount is debited (subtracted) from the payer's account and credited (added) to the payee's account.

compound interest: Interest calculated not only on the original principal, but also on the interest already accrued.

co-signer: The person who signs on a credit agreement in addition to the primary applicant. This person is legally responsible for repayment of the debt.

credit: In business, buying or borrowing on the promise to repay at a later date. In any credit arrangement, there is a creditor (a person, bank, store, or company to whom money is owed) and a debtor (the person who owes money). In bookkeeping, credit is a sum of money owed to an individual or institution.

credit bureau: An agency that checks credit information and keeps a complete file on people who apply for and use credit.

credit card: A plastic card that gives access to a line of credit. Users are limited in how much they can charge, but they are not required to repay the full amount each month. Instead the balance accrues interest with only a minimum payment due.

credit limit: The maximum amount of money a borrower can access in a credit account.

credit rating: A financial institution's evaluation of whether a person is suitable to receive credit. Credit ratings are based on an individual's character, capacity to repay, and capital.

credit report: A summary of a consumer's credit usage, including payment histories and current status of all credit accounts. This report plays a large part in the decision to grant credit to a consumer.

credit union: A member-owned financial institution, either provincially or federally chartered. Credit unions are often more competitive than banks and savings and loan associations because their nonprofit status makes their operating costs lower.

currency: Money; anything used as a common medium of exchange. In practice, currency means cash, particularly paper money. Bankers often use the phrase "coin and currency" to refer to cents and dollars.

debit: A bookkeeping term for a sum of money owed by an individual or institution; a charge deducted from an account.

debit card: A banking card enhanced with ATM (automated teller machine) and POS (point-of-sale) features that can be used to purchase goods and services electronically. The card replaces cash or checks. Transactions are deducted from the cardholder's checking account either immediately or within one to three days. Depending upon the type of card, a debit card may require the user to sign his or her name or enter a PIN (personal identification number) into special equipment.

default: A status assigned to a cardholder if he or she fails to perform or conform to all the items listed in the cardholder agreement.

deposit slip: An itemized slip showing the exact amount of paper money, coin, and checks being deposited to a particular account.

depositor: An individual or company that puts money in a bank account.

endorse: To sign, as the payee, the back of a check before cashing, depositing, or giving it to someone else. The first endorsement must be made by the payee to authorize the transaction. Later endorsements may be made by whoever receives the check.

interest: The fee paid for the use of money. Interest may be paid, for example, by an individual to a bank for credit card use, or by a bank to an individual for holding a savings account. Interest is expressed in terms of annual percentage rate (APR).

introductory rate: A temporarily low interest rate, used as incentive to entice a consumer to sign up for credit. After the introductory period, the rate will increase to the standard percentage.

joint account: A savings or checking account established in the names of more than one person (e.g., parent/child, wife/husband).

late payment fee: A fee charged to a consumer if his or her monthly payment is made after the due date stated on the billing statement.

liabilities: Money owed to individuals, businesses, or institutions.

line of credit: An authorized amount of credit given to an individual, business, or institution.

market economy: An economic system permitting an open exchange of goods and services between producers and consumers, such as is found in Canada.

minimum payment: The smallest payment a consumer can make in a billing cycle to keep the account from going into default.

money: Anything generally recognized as a medium of exchange.

mortgage: A long-term loan obtained by individuals to buy a home that legally transfers ownership from the debtor to the creditor until the debt is paid.

overdraft: A check written for more money than is currently in the account. If the bank refuses to cash the check, it is said to have bounced.

passbook: A booklet given by the bank to the depositor to record deposits, withdrawals, and interest earned on a savings account.

personal identification number (PIN): A code that provides security for consumers at an ATM.

point of sale (POS): The store or other location where a transaction takes place.

prime rate: An index rate that is used to determine the APR in a variable interest rate account.

principal: The original amount of money borrowed, deposited, or invested before interest accrues.

proprietary credit card: A private labelled credit card typically issued by a department store or petroleum company that can only be used at those specific outlets.

savings account: A bank account that accrues interest in exchange for use of the money on deposit.

service charge: A monthly fee a bank charges for handling a checking account.

stop payment: A request made to a bank to not pay a specific check. If requested soon enough, the check will not be debited from the payer's account. Normally there is a charge for this service.

terms: The period of time and the interest rate arranged between creditor and debtor to repay a loan.

transaction date: The date that a purchase was made or a cash advance was taken.

wire transfer: A transaction that electronically transfers money from one financial institution to another.

withdrawal: An amount of money taken out of an account.

APPENDIX A

TWO FREE TICKETS TO A KIDS RIDE TO RICHES SEMINAR

If you enjoyed this book, you will love our seminars!

This book is your ticket to a Kids Ride to Riches seminar.

Register for two complimentary tickets (one adult, one child) at www.kidsridetoriches.com.

Enter this code: **Become Rich 243**

We look forward to assisting you and your family on the ride to riches.

Seminars are scheduled in the Greater Toronto area during 2009 and then offered in other major cities in Canada and the United States at the end of 2009. Please check the website for specific dates and cities.

APPENDIX B

ANSWER KEY

ACTIVITY: MY FAMILY'S FINANCIAL AWARENESS

1. What percent of people worry about money every day?

   b. 70 percent

2. What percent of people live paycheck to paycheck?

   c. 66 percent

3. Do people save more or less money now than ten years ago?

   a. Less

4. The use of savings accounts is more prevalent in _____ than the _____.

   d. Canada; the United States

5. Children learn saving and spending habits from _____.

   a. Parents and grandparents

6. How are budgeting and money management skills normally learned?

   b. By trial and error

7. At what age should children begin to learn about money management and the importance of savings accounts?

   d. All of the above

8. Money in your savings account is primarily meant to pay for:

   e. b and c (Investments to make more money and specific goals (college) or large purchases (car))

9. You should pay your bills first and then see what is left over to save.

   b. False

10. How can you best *begin* making investments?

   c. Use money from a savings account.

11. Why is it important to learn money management
    skills early in life?

    e. All of the above

12. Why is it important to set goals?

    d. All of the above

13. How can reading this book help you and your family?

    Although all of the answers to this question are true, the
    last one is the most important because money management
    is not part of our schools' curriculum, so we have to take
    responsibility to teach and learn together.

14. People are:

    a. Born rich

    b. Become rich

    e. Smart workers if they become rich

    g. Rich if they create a mind-set of being rich

How Have You **BECOME A RICHER YOU?**

Write Doug Meharg and Let Him Know!

doug@kidsridetoriches.com

You Were Born Rich

Bob Proctor
ISBN 978-0-9656264-1-5

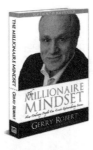

The Millionaire Mindset
*How Ordinary People Can
Create Extraordinary Income*

Gerry Robert
ISBN 978-1-59930-030-6

Rekindle The Magic In
Your Relationship
Making Love Work

Anita Jackson
ISBN 978-1-59930-041-2

Finding The Bloom of
The Cactus Generation
*Improving the quality of
life for Seniors*

Maggie Walters
ISBN 978-1-59930-011-5

The Beverly Hills Shape
The Truth About Plastic Surgery

Dr. Stuart Linder
ISBN 978-1-59930-049-8

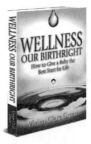

Wellness Our Birthright
*How to give a baby the best
start in life.*

Vivien Clere Green
ISBN 978-1-59930-020-7

Lighten Your Load

Peter Field
ISBN 978-1-59930-000-9

Change & How To
Survive In The New
Economy
*7 steps to finding freedom
& escaping the rat race*

Barrie Day
ISBN 978-1-59930-015-3

OTHER BOOKS FROM LIFESUCCESS PUBLISHING

Stop Singing The Blues
*10 Powerful Strategies For
Hitting The High Notes In
Your Life*

Dr. Cynthia Barnett
ISBN 978-1-59930-022-1

Don't Be A Victim,
*Protect Yourself
Everything Seniors Need To
Know To Avoid Being Taken
Financially*

Jean Ann Dorrell
ISBN 978-1-59930-024-5

A "Hand Up", not a
"Hand Out"
*The best ways to help others
help themselves*

David Butler
ISBN 978-1-59930-071-9

Doctor, Your Medicine Is
Killing Me!
*One Man's Journey from
Near Death to Health
and Wellness*

Pete Coussa
ISBN 978-1-59930-047-4

I Believe in Me
*7 Ways for Woman to Step
Ahead in Confidence*

Lisa Gorman
ISBN 978-1-59930-069-6

The Color of Success
*Why Color Matters in your
Life, your Love, your Lexus*

Mary Ellen Lapp
ISBN 978-1-59930-078-8

If Not Now, When?
What's Your Dream?

Cindy Nielsen
ISBN 978-1-59930-073-3

The Skills to Pay the
Bills… and then some!
*How to inspire everyone in
your organisation into high
performance!*

Buki Mosaku
ISBN 978-1-59930-058-0

The Secret To Cracking
The Property Code
*7 Timeless Principles for
Successful Real Estate
Investment*

Richard S.G. Poole
ISBN 978-1-59930-063-4

Why My Mother Didn't
Want Me To Be Psychic
*The Intelligent Guide To The
Sixth Sense*

Heidi Sawyer
ISBN 978-1-59930-052-8

The Make It Happen Man
*10 ways to turn obstacles
into stepping stones without
breaking a sweat*

Dean Storer
ISBN 978-1-59930-077-1

Change your body
Change your life
*with the Fittest Couple in
the World*

Matt Thom &
Monica Wright
ISBN 978-1-59930-065-8

Good Vibrations!
*Can you tune in to a more
positive life?*

Clare Tonkin
ISBN 978-1-59930-064-1

The Millionaire Genius
*How to wake up the money
magic within you.*

David Ogunnaike
ISBN 978-1-59930-026-9

Scoring Eagles
*Improve Your Score In Golf,
Business and Life*

Max Carbone
ISBN 978-1-59930-045-0

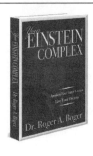

The Einstein Complex
*Awaken your inner genius,
live your dream.*

Dr. Roger A. Boger
ISBN 978-1-59930-055-9

OTHER BOOKS FROM LIFESUCCESS PUBLISHING

P.A.T.C.H.
*5 Strategies to living
your life with purpose.*

Alan W. Goff
ISBN # 978-1-59930-100-6

WE *the new* Me
*Unleash the Creative
Power of Your Mind*

Debbii McKoy
ISBN # 978-159930104--4

The Sweet Smell of Success
Health & Wealth Secrets

James "Tad" Geiger M.D.
ISBN # 978-1-59930-088-7

Living the Law of
Attraction
*Real Stories of People
Manifesting Wealth,
Health and Happiness*

Rich German, Andy Wong
& Robin Hoch
ISBN # 978-1-59930-091-7

Wealth Matters
Abundance is Your Birthlight

Chris J. Snook with
Chet Snook
ISBN # 978-1-59930-096-2

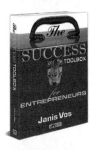

The Success Toolbox
For Entrepreneurs

Janis Vos
ISBN # 978-1-59930-005-4

Home Sense
*Dealing with the Trauma
of Renovating your Home*

John Salton
ISBN # 978-1-59930-169-3

The Girlz Guide to
Building Wealth
...and men like it too

Maya Galletta, Aaron
Cohen, Polly McCormick,
Mike McCormick
ISBN # 978-1-59930-048-1